GROOM *an* APPEALING PERSONALITY

Prof. P.A.Varghese

PUSTAK MAHAL®

Publishers
Pustak Mahal®

Administrative office and sale centre

J-3/16 , Daryaganj, New Delhi-110002
☎ 23276539, 23272783, 23272784 • *Fax:* 011-23260518
E-mail: info@pustakmahal.com • *Website:* www.pustakmahal.com

Branches

Bengaluru: ☎ 080-22234025 • *Telefax:* 080-22240209
E-mail: pustakmahalblr@gmail.com
Mumbai: ☎ 022-22010941, 022-22053387
E-mail: unicornbooksmumbai@gmail.com

ISBN 978-81-223-1659-9

Edition: 2018

Printed at : Ar Emm International,

Contents

❖❖

Introduction

Have you ever thought why some people have lots of friends while others do not? Why some are climbing up the ladder so effortlessly while others remain at the lower or middle rungs? Why are some welcome in any group while others have to lead a lonely life?

The difference is largely due to the type of personalities these people have.

While some people are likeable, well-mannered, ambitious, smart, healthy with articulate communicative ability, others are negative, unhealthy, least interested in dressing and grooming and difficult to deal with. Try to observe parties and you will notice how those who are confident, always smiling and going out of their way to talk with others are the life of the party, while there are those who prefer to stay in one corner, all by their lonesome selves.

People have different characteristics that are reflected in their social and interpersonal interactions with others. Some are:

- sociable and enthusiastic;
- friendly and kind;
- organized and hardworking;
- calm and tranquil;
- intellectual and creative.

There are those who are not sociable, friendly, organized, hardworking, intelligent or calm. These five personality dimensions provide a very broad overview of one's character. Most people's personality is a combination of each of these personality characteristics. For example, someone can be highly social, hardworking and extremely creative but unfriendly and highly emotional. Any number of permutation and combination is possible with these characteristics. Someone who is high in Intellect and sociable can be creative, witty and humorous. On the other hand, one who is high in Intellect but low in sociability will be more reflective. A few are neither intelligent, agreeable nor sociable. A number of us are highly sensitive, hot tempered and impulsive although intelligent.

Whatever these combinations and permutations are, your personality sends out a signal that others read and respond accordingly. Hence, it is all the more crucial that we develop a positive, capable and dynamic personality.

There are researchers who maintain that personality is stable throughout life depending on one's early childhood experiences, education, profession and marriage. Making people understand that they can develop or improve their personality is not all that easy. Sometimes it is an overwhelming task as many feel they cannot improve their personality at all. Anyone who is sane can take command of his personality and develop it the way he wants to. There are many new concepts and techniques available now which are laid out before you in this book to help you do it.

This book has been written for those who suffer from personality problems and for those who want to polish it. You have the potential in you to change your personality for the better. You may have good IQ, good emotional set-up, good education, good health and so on enabling you to take your personality to higher levels.

You need first to desire and dream to change it for the better. Probably that is why you are reading this book. You can easily develop a better one by knocking off the rough edges, polishing the rusted parts, and making the whole appearance shine. You need to change your thought patterns and beliefs too. Now that you are having this book in your hand, you are close to achieving your dream. Maybe you need to upgrade your dressing a little, change your body language into a confident one, change your internal communications, thought patterns and limiting beliefs. Fix an aim in your life and go after it persistently; reframe unpleasant experiences and adopt confidence-building techniques in your postures.

If Only...

You may be thinking: 'If only I was born in a better home; if only I could get a better university education; if only I was luckier; if only I had more wealth; if only I was better-looking.... Even with all these you may not be able to develop a better personality unless you really want to. The first and foremost requisite is to have a strong desire to improve the way you look and the way you are. There may be many who sincerely want to develop their personalities; when it's their long cherished dream, they will eventually find ways to improve it.

This book guides you how to develop your personality in a simple and straight forward manner. Thirty-nine personality development principles are set out here that will enable you to become pleasant, elegant, smart and communicative. This book is filled to the brim with the tried and tested techniques on personality development. Start your great journey now to become more communicative with a vibrant, confident, pleasant and a likeable personality.

This is a road map to becoming a better, successful, pleasant, confident and ambitious person who is welcomed in any group. If you desire a better personality, here is a practical guide. But simply reading it won't help you at all. It's a practical guide with proven and tested techniques and methods. If you decide to put them into practise, we'll meet through these pages.

India requires people with highly developed personalities to man its corporates, and government offices. We need leaders at all social levels. Highly developed personality is a must for all of them and this book is an all-embracing personality development guide.

Suppose there is a remarkable guide that will lift you up from failure to success, from inferiority to confidence, from negativity to positivity; from boring to a pleasing nature, from illness to health, from being clumsy to being fit, from being ugly to becoming smart, from doubt to self-assurance. This book is intended to be such a guide.

At the outset let me congratulate you and assure you that your goals can easily be achieved. By reading and applying the techniques outlined here, I guarantee you will become a pleasant, likeable, confident and smart person.

The book you hold now is an easy-to-follow tool, fun to read and easy to follow. It's a 'how to book.' Spend a few minutes thumbing through the book to get familiar with the flow of ideas. Then read the book more carefully, understanding and assimilating each and every principle and practical tip. Study the techniques of each chapter; assimilate them and start to put them into practise. This book has been designed to be user-friendly and with valuable suggestions. It also has quotes and practical tips in each page. Let them help you develop a magnetic and highly efficient personality. Good luck and enjoyable reading!

— Prof. P.A.Varghese
Kochi, Ph:-9895471704
Email:professorpavarghese@yahooc.o.uk

Chapter-1

Personality and personality development defined

Everybody's heard the term 'personality,' and you probably have some idea of your own personality type — *outgoing/reserved, sensitive/shy or strong*. Psychologists point out to the individual differences in the way people tend to think, feel and behave.

An individual's personality normally refers to his/her *appearance, characteristics, attitude, mindset and behaviour* with others.

Every individual has his own characteristic way of behaving, responding to situations, emotions, and perceiving things and looking at the world. No two individuals are similar or same. One might like going out for parties and socializing while another might simply sit at home and read a book or hear his favourite songs. One might be very sensitive and react immediately in an emotional way while another might be patient, cool and has a measured or calculated response. One might like to be fashionable and go after the trend, while another is OK in his classic style and ways. People are different or each person has a different personality.

If you are too shy to speak in a group, you lack self-esteem and confidence. If your relationship with your family is not all that good, it only means you lack communicative ability, empathy, ability to develop trust and you are unwilling to make others happy. How you deal with your spouse, parents, or children has something to do with the kind of person you are. Although family members will love you, there are times when problems arise, and how you deal with each one affects the relationships. All these can be changed if you strive to improve and develop yourself.

Personality defined

You can find different definitions for it in the dictionary and elsewhere.

The word personality itself comes from the Latin word persona, which is referred to as a theatrical mask-work by Roman performers in order to either project different roles or disguise their identities. A brief definition would be that personality is made up of the characteristic patterns of thoughts, feelings and behaviours that distinguish individuals from one another or which make a person unique.

The simple definition points out to a combination of characteristics or qualities that form an individual's distinctive character. We say she has a **pleasant and sunny personality or he is a vibrant and cheerful person.**

Almost every day we describe and assess the personalities of the people around us. Whether we realize it or not, we observe how people behave and how this behaviour affects our relationship to them.

So what exactly makes up a personality? As described in the definition above, you would expect that traits and patterns of thought, emotions and behaviour make up an important part.

Personality development is the development of the organized pattern of behaviours, attitudes and thoughts that make a person distinctive.

But when we come in contact with a person, the following points are consciously or unconsciously observed:

- His/her dressing and grooming, colour, body shape and facial features, the way he/she stands or walks and the way he holds his head, arms and other limbs.
- We note the way he greets us or shake-hands. Is the shake-hand firm, cold or lifeless?
- Does he/she smile?
- Is the greeting warm or perfunctory?
- How does he/she move? Is he slow or brisk?
- Is he clear, brief, articulate and convincing when he speaks?

We immediately make an opinion about a person. We sometimes say in our mind, ***a good, smart guy or a beautiful lively woman.*** At other times, we get the feeling he/she is awkward or reserved and even shy. This influences our further interactions and future relationship with him/her.

A pleasing personality is one that has warmth in his countenance, balance in behaviour and is moderate in his or her reactions in public and at home, simultaneously maintaining a friendly, approachable and sensible behaviour towards people.

Easily recognizable personality traits

- Each one has generally a recognizable order and regularity to his/her behaviour. Essentially, same people act in the same ways or similar ways in a variety of situations.
- One's personality not only influences us to behave in a certain way or in a certain situation but it actually causes that behaviour.
- One's personality is reflected in his/her thoughts, beliefs, feelings, close relationships and other social interactions.
- Personality also means the way you dress and groom up, your body language, manners, behaviour, and ways of communication.

Why do you do what you do?

- Your personality determines it. How you will react to a given situation or cope up with it, is largely based on how you have been formed. We should be able to exert control on what happens in our life and thus try to better our life. We should attempt to control our behaviour in a positive manner, and improve our life, never try consciously or unconsciously to make it worse. Let us aim at a better quality of life through a better personal understanding as to who we are and how can we acquire a better personality.

Environmental factors, family background, financial conditions, genetics, situations and circumstances—all contribute to an individual's personality.

There are a number of different theories about how personality develops. It is not our purpose here to go into such theoretical details but we will be examining how can we develop a personality that propels us forward in our career, social life, at home and outside.

What an individual experiences in his early childhood and growing days shapes his personality along with his genetic set-up. Personality traits may emerge early but they can be changed throughout one's life. Although almost 50% of variation in observable personality traits is attributable to genetic influences, the other 50% comes from environment, experiences and our own interferences.

Why are you the way you are?

Your genes (from father, mother and their parents) determine your body-physiology, looks, general appearance, and to a large extent your biology. Genes from parents also determine some of your mental traits too. Your genetic makeup has a large role in determining why you behave as you do. While genes do not determine behaviour, they play a role in what we do and why you do it.

Our early childhood or home environment, our parents and close relatives and how they behaved to us; school and early friends all go in making our personal traits. But they are not deterministic. We can change, adopt, evolve and become a better person. Humans have that great ability but the sad part is very few of us make use of this inherent capability.

Genetics and environment in our behaviour: These two factors have strong influence on behaviour, and it is largely believed that human behaviour is an intricate result of the interplay of the two. Experts maintain that our genes influence the way we respond to our environment, and at the same time the expression of our genes is changed by the environment around us; therefore, the relationship between genetic and environmental influences cannot be easily separated.

In a layman's language, our day-to-day lives reflect our personality. Genetic set-up, family background, upbringing, and so on determine our behaviour. An individual with a troubled childhood would not open up easily or he may become an introvert. One who was loved, and brought up healthily would not have problems in interacting with others and to lead a meaningful social and professional life. You really can't blame one for being an introvert or a shy person. It's not due to their mistakes that some are diffident or experience inferiority complex. Genes and family background have shaped them. There are many who suffer from personality disorders for which they may not be responsible at all. There is hope for all. Anyone can shred off their unwanted traits and develop healthy aspects of personality.

Factors needed in shaping one's personality

Heredity – As already mentioned, parental genes determine or greatly influence an individual's personality like physique, appearance, body type, complexion, IQ, emotional levels, one's biology and so on.

Environment – The environment to which one is subjected to during his growing years plays an important role in determining his/her personality. Different cultures, family backgrounds, parents – all have a crucial role in shaping one's personalities.

Situation – An individual's personality also changes with current circumstances and situations. One would behave in a different way in a different context. Behaviour is very much contextual.

There is still a controversy as to which factor ranks higher in affecting personality development. All experts agree that ***high-quality parenting*** plays a critical role in the development of a child's personality. Parents who know how to adept their parenting approach to the particular temperament of their child can best provide guidance and ensure the successful development of their child's personality.

Is one's personality set?

Absolutely, no. *Genetics, early childhood and growing years' experiences have influenced you. But you have the freedom and capability to mould and change your personality for the better.* There are so many who suffer from being shy, being introvert, being unorganized, being hot-tempered and so on. This is where the role of personality development comes in.

In their best-selling publication 'Born to Win' well-known psychologists Muriel and Dorothy have written that a man is basically born to win. But due to negligence, our winning potential doesn't grow to the best of its capacity. Mostly people develop their personality according to their genes, upbringing, early social experiences and parental expectations. Therefore, they are unable to develop to the fullest extent their unique traits and potentialities. It is up to us now to break free of these barriers and rise up bravely to a great unique individual. Only thus can one transform his ordinary personality into an impressive one.

- It was previously thought that every person lived his or her whole life according to the personality script written in childhood. None could change it. Years of research and practical applications have changed that perception.
- With the help of simple methods now anybody can develop a winning personality and change his or her future. This book provides you some simple ways to improve your personality.

Personality severe disorders. Some people have great difficulty dealing with other people. They tend to be inflexible, rigid, and unable to respond to the changes and normal stresses of life and find it very difficult for them to participate in social activities. When these characteristics are present in one to an extreme and if they are persistently interfering with healthy development, a diagnostic evaluation with a licensed physician or mental health professional may become necessary. The following simple personality development methods may not help them much.

Personality development

It is well-known that some people become successful and some do not. What makes one person succeed and another fail? The answer to this can be found in his personality traits. Your personality decides your success or failure in life as it decides the type of thoughts you have which then decides the type of your actions. Your personality decides whether you will be more likely to succeed or less likely to do so. Hence there is an urgency to develop your personality to a suitable level.

Personality development can be summed up as: It is improvement in all aspects of an individual's life—in dress, body language, be it with friends, in the office, at home or in any other environment. People skills are an integral part of it too. We have to deprogramme some of the negative beliefs we have been holding with us for long and put in place the positive ones. Thought patterns do influence the way we approach life and conduct ourselves in our day-to-day lives.

Corporations are looking for pleasing personality and a simultaneous good performance capability in a perfect candidate. The individual who has mastered the art of social tact, or the guy who has learned and developed the social set of skills necessary today, has a lot of benefits that will help him for long. Charm, sociable and affable attributes, warmth and the right attitude and good behaviour makes one stand out in any crowd. It is obvious that every individual can be greatly benefitted through personality development.

If you are always well-dressed, outgoing and sociable, agreeable and pleasant, having a number of positive friends and acquaintances, displaying good body language, being positive, physically fit & healthy, full of energy and enthusiasm, action-oriented, with an ability to control emotions and impulses, professionally successful, enjoying family and social life, with good communicative ability, coping with setbacks and failures in life.... then you have a great personality. You will climb up professionally and in personal lives with ease.

Personality and career success

These are intertwined. Your personality will dictate success or failure in your career. In the workplace, your promotion or popularity depends on how you conduct yourself in your job and how you deal with your superiors, colleagues and friends. Staying diligent and focused on the job at hand, maintaining good relationships with your bosses and all others ensure success. Though majority of us have the mental capacity to handle the responsibilities bestowed on us, we lack a level of emotional intelligence to maintain good relationships and move happily with all.

In other words, high IQ and willingness to put in long focused hours are not enough to succeed in the work place. You need EQ, ability to cope up with the stress, pulls and strains of the work place and deal with your competing colleagues and demanding superiors. You need to control your emotions not to overreact and have calculated measured responses.

As you might be well-aware of, emotional intelligence and personality go hand in hand. This is why personality development holds a very vital role in a person's ability to succeed in whatever career he chooses to take. If you are easily frustrated, without the capability to handle stress brought about by work-related events, then it will be easy for you to quit during difficult times. Then you will find out another job. Here also stressful situations will arise and your inability to cope up with them will see you going out. Knowing how to relate with others and how to handle stressful situations are all part of the personality development course.

No matter how ordinary we think we are, we can polish our traits and behaviours to a shining level. We can transform our personality into one that aims to succeed in any aspect of our lives.

Developing one's own personality will address the problems we face both at home and at work and help us become successful in every endeavour we engage ourselves in.

- **It is never too late to change.** No matter how young or old you are, whatever level you may be in your career, you can still do something to achieve a better, more desirable personality.
- **The ability to perform well in public and to make an impression on people** with your social skills and as a good person, maintaining your own identity, is something that will take you a long way up in life.

Personality development is easily possible with the right means and methods. One can always develop one's personality by learning and can develop it with experience and practise. One has to keep updating it too. Old ways have to be discarded and new trends adopted as society, social norms and dress codes all evolve and develop. Only with constant updates, can one keep up with the trends that are changing like whirlwinds every now and then.

The process starts right from one's childhood. It is shaped afterwards on the basis of the impact of various positive and negative life situations and challenges and other factors in life. It is continuously being evolved and one should always keep on improving his/her personality to meet and overcome the challenges of the outside world more effectively and efficiently.

- Regardless of what your personality is now, it can develop and evolve.
- If you don't direct this evolution and change, it may go astray and your personality will degenerate into something undesirable.
- With conscious interferences, you can still do something about your personality today and improve it, polish or make it effective.

This book is intended to help young and old, professionals and laymen, students and teachers, housewives and girls to acquire a better personality by effecting small changes in one's thinking, health habits, dressing and grooming, body language, communication and approach to life. Its methods are laid out in a cogent and simple style for all to easily adopt and assimilate. We deal with how one can look better, become confident, healthier and improve ways of communication. Effort has been made to make each topic interesting and inspiring to the reader.

Personality development is improving the way we think, feel, behave and carry ourselves. It is not confined to the improvement of a single aspect; rather it is about improving our whole person as an entity with a cluster of qualities helping to present oneself in a better way personality.

Chapter-2

Why should you develop your personality?

Personality development grooms an individual and helps him make a mark in life. Individuals need to have their own style. There is no need to blindly follow or copy others. You need to be unique and if possible set an example for people around. Personality development makes you look good and presentable and it helps you face the world with a smile.

It encourages individuals to look at the brighter sides of life. A positive attitude will help one face even the worst situations with a smile. A genuine smile will melt away half of your problems and help evaporate your stress and worries. There is no point worrying about minor issues and problems.

An individual with a negative attitude finds a problem in every situation. Rather than worrying and criticizing people around, go into the situation, analyze it and try to find an appropriate solution for the same. Remember, if there is a problem, there has to be a solution as well. Personality development helps you enhence a positive attitude in life.

Individuals have to behave well with people around. One cannot be rude to any one how low a position he occupies or how low a work he does. One has to be polite and nice to all. Being polite with others will make you popular among people and they will in turn respect you. You can't demand respect from anyone through arrogance or rudeness. Personality development plays an important role in polishing your outer and inner sides.

Unless an individual has a magnetic power to attract others towards him, he will be a loner and a sad person.

We are social animals. We need to interact with people around. We in fact need them for our own happiness and well-being. One needs to develop the stamp of charisma—a personal power that brings others to you. Personality development helps you gain recognition and acceptance from the society as well as people around.

It goes without saying that personality development plays an important role in an individual's professional and personal lives. One needs to be:

- disciplined;
- well-mannered;
- courteous;
- punctual;
- honest;
- with a flexible attitude;
- willing to learn;
- of friendly nature;
- eager to help others.

Never hesitate to share information with others. One needs to be an asset to his/her organization. An unorganized individual finds it difficult to climb the ladder of success to be the fittest to survive.

Personality development teaches you:

- to respect your boss, colleagues, family members, friends, neighbours, relatives and so on;
- it will teach you never to make fun of or criticize anyone at the workplace;
- not to be rude to others;
- not to carry his/her personal grudges to work place.

Personality development lessons will help you differentiate between your personal as well as professional life. It is really essential to keep a balance between both the lives to lead a peaceful and stress free life. Always reach office on time. Some people have a tendency to work till late. Late sittings not only increase your stress levels but also spoil your personal life. Sitting till late at the office indicates that an individual is extremely poor in time management skills.

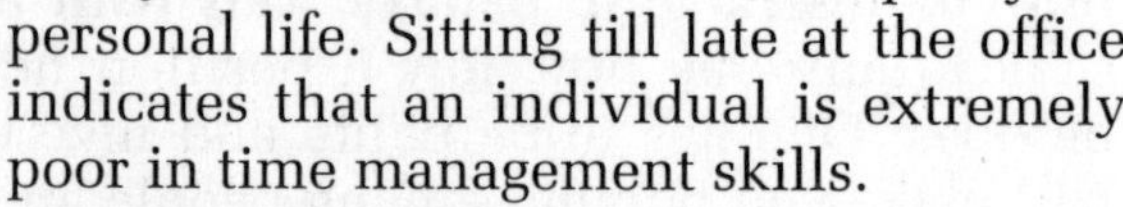

Personality development will help you develop an impressive personality and make you stand apart from the rest. It also plays an essential role in improving one's communication skills. We should be able to master the art of expressing our thoughts and feelings in the most efficient way. All these together will make an individual a confident one well-appreciated and respected person wherever he goes.

Personality development is the need of the hour as it is required for our all-round development and to succeed in this competitive world and to win the race of life. Each person has a different character and personality that can be developed, polished and refined.

Personality development focuses on the enhancement and grooming of one's outer and inner self to bring about a positive change in one's life. Personality development is for the growth and development of thoughts, emotions, appearance, attitude, nature, communication skills, behaviour and activities that make you unique and successful in life. It is a tool to bring out one's abilities and powers to make him more confident to face the outside world and succeed in whatever endeavour one has chosen in life.

This process includes:

- boosting and enhancing one's confidence;
- improving communication and speaking abilities;
- expanding the boundaries of thinking and knowledge;
- developing new hobbies or skills;
- adding style and elegance to one's looks and walks;
- adopting fine etiquettes and manners;
- cultivating positivity;
- cultivating liveliness;
- learning to cultivate a grateful mind;
- learning to be nice to one and all;
- making your appearance;
- making your behaviour better at home and at the work place;
- making you successful in life;
- making you bring out and polish your inherent talents.

Your personality develops whether you like it or not. It will go the way it is pulled by your friends, interests, family, career and sometimes it may land you up in difficulty.

We need to develop our personality in a conscious way directing it all the time after understanding ourselves so that we gain more confidence, acceptance in society, work place and eventually succeed in life.

If you let life just blow this way or that way, how will you achieve what you yearn in life?

One needs to develop one's personality to take in ups and downs and to expand oneself. You have to exercise your bodies and your minds; you should develop your appearance and cultivate positive ways to face life.

Try to improve yourself in some way, whether it is appearance, communication, manners, being likeable; let us practise to get better at something. Let us always try to be stretching ourselves in some new way to stay up and not to get beaten down by life. You can be your own person but improve yourself each day a wee-bit. It is not what you are now that matters but what you aim at and how you conduct yourself to reach there.

Your personality can be moulded into what you have always wanted. You can attain a winning personality which everyone will admire you for.

You need to be aware of your present: To groom your personality, you need take into account the following points:

- body language;
- thoughts and aims;
- how you spend your time;
- how you behave to others;
- your level of health and fitness;
- your appearance;
- your habits;
- your willingness to give;
- your helping nature;
- the way you drive;
- the type of friends you have;
- how you deal with your family;
- your life at the work place.

Look at yourself in the mirror while you talk, and notice every form of body language you portray—the way you stand, hold your head, eyes, arms and legs. Are these positive? If they are negative, make an effort to eliminate them.

1. Have you set up an aim in life and do you align your thoughts to achieve it? What care do you give to improve your health? What stuff do you eat on a regular basis? Are they harmful or good for your body? Is your intake more/less/just right? Are you fit, agile and flexible? Is your weight and height matching?

2. Do you take care of your appearance? Do you know your appearance 'talks'? In a few seconds, people assess you and give marks for the way you present yourself. What extra effort do you put in to become smart and confident?

3. Are you nice to one and all–irrespective of whether he is big or small, influential or not, relative or stranger. Are you rude to ordinary people like salesmen, waiters, pump attendants and others? Give respect and take it. You cannot demand respect.

4. How do you treat your family members? Do they enjoy your presence with them? Do you do everything possible to make each of them happy and satisfied?

5. Do you follow the rules of the road while you drive? Are you a rude driver shouting and yelling at co-drivers? Are you concerned about

others, their safety and happiness? Are you willing to give way and wait for your turn?

6. Are you willing to help others, share their problems and listen empathetically? Do you help the needy and the poor –do you give out a part of your earnings for charity?
7. Do you follow etiquette and manners? Do you eat with your mouth open and make noise? Are you careful while standing in the queue and wait for your turn? Do you follow manners in a restaurant, party and in other public places?
8. How is your work place? Do you enjoy your job, boss and your colleagues? Do you work to live or work more than you are expected to? Are you focused while you carry out your duties? Do you take extra care to be nice to customers, vendors and salesmen?
9. What type of friends do you have? Are they positive and ambitious ones trying to go up in life? Are they pessimists –criticizing others, finding fault with life and engaged in rumour mongering? Do you try to make more friends everywhere?

It is recommended that you practise positive body language so that in the course of time your body language becomes natural to you. Once you go through the chapter on body language you will be aware of the good and negative ways, you can easily figure out which ones you need to get used to and which ones you need to get rid of. And little by little, on a daily basis, you need to practise and maintain good body language. Constantly remind yourself of good gestures, movements, and facial expressions you should have until they will become innate with you.

In order to go up the ladder you need to enhance your knowledge base, set aims, cultivate more friends, make your family happy, follow etiquette and manners in each setting, focus on a job you enjoy and have a helping attitude to others on your journey. There are plenty of tips in each page of this book to help and guide you along the more acceptable and better ways. If your personality is not polished up, refined, made sharper and effective, your life will not be as enjoyable, successful or happy in each stage of life.

With a pleasant personality, you can get along well with people everywhere. This programme of personality development aims at building a better person, a better human being. It is aimed to improve your overall behaviour, build your mental ability, physical build with better emotional control, better communication skills, and pleasing manners.

Your personality is what you think and feel and you can change your personality by changing your thinking and feeling. Learn to think the way you want to think, feel the way you want to feel. Think what you want to become and you will become it. This book will help you to think right.

Start thinking positive from now

- I am attractive, elegant and confident;
- I am ambitious and hardworking;
- I am friendly and assertive;
- I am good, careful, and caring;
- I am moderate, calm and composed;
- I am pleasant, peaceful and cheerful;
- I am kind and happy;
- I am polite and considerate;
- I am reliable and fair;
- I am winning and victorious.

Contrary to what you may think, you can improve your personality. Until recently, it was believed that personality is permanent. In 1890, William James, the famous Harvard psychologist, wrote in his book, The Principles of Psychology, that personality was "set in plaster" by early adulthood. This view prevailed for over a century; however, the idea that personality is more fluid has gained ground over time. We now realize that we have influence and control over the traits and characteristics we want to develop or refine.

Chapter-3

Know thyself

"Know thyself is the beginning of all wisdom."

—Aristotle

Successful people are Self-Aware! One has to find out exactly what he needs to enhance his personality.

Landmark studies in western universities have revealed that 83% of high performers scored high in Self-Awareness. **Self-knowledge is critical to your personality and professional success**. To become self-aware, you need to invent your assets and liabilities, and identify how to improve yourself. One needs to start with taking a good look at oneself, analyzing his/her traits, the strengths and weaknesses and everything that needs to be worked upon. Don't shy away from accepting your flaws and learn about yourself as much as you can.

Hence, before you embark on your journey to strengthen your personality, know yourself.

We were pure like a dew drop when we were born and our mind was blank. As time passed, we were subjected to stimuli, experiences, impressions that shaped our personality with its defenses, limiting beliefs, ego inferiority complex and confidence levels. These engrained impressions shaped our perceptions and made us what we are today.

Aware that life will not last forever, we ask ourselves:

- who am I?
- why am I here?
- what is my emotional set-up?

- where am I going?
- am I living my life on my terms?
- am I living my life as others expect me to?
- what are the flaws in my personality?

Studies have estimated that 95% of what we do, think and say is unconscious. Become conscious of what is now unconscious - and this will help transform your life. Self-awareness is a pre-requisite in any programme to develop oneself.

Your self-image is the way you see yourself. It is the self you think you are. But often your self-image can be deceptive. There can be many undesirable traits lying unnoticed in your inner self. They have to be brought forward for correcting yourself. How well do you really know yourself?

- What unique gifts, talents and skills do you bring to this world? Can you list them down?
- What makes you fail often or meet with obstacles on your paths? Mention at least 5 reasons now.
- How much of your life is consciously controlled by you? Is it just going on unaware?
- What gives you meaning and purpose for your life? Can you specify it?
- Do you have a personal development plan for the future?If yes, note it down here.

You will have to assess the strength of your thoughts, feelings and behaviour to others too. When you answer each one of these questions below you will know whether you are emotional, confident, self-centred, social, charismatic, leader, follower, thinker, doer, giver, outgoing, extrovert, introvert, organized, honest , tidy and so on.

Now think over the following:

- Are you a likeable person?
- Are you self-centred?
- Do you think you are physically attractive?
- Are you a hard worker?
- Do you day-dream too much?
- Are you careful in dressing and grooming?
- Do you keep an upright and confident posture while sitting, standing and moving?
- Do you feel comfortable around people?
- Do you find it difficult to approach strangers?
- Are you shy in groups?
- Do you like to go for parties?

- Are you careful in following good social manners?
- Do you make friends easily?
- Do you gossip a lot?
- Do you behave to others politely and with concern?
- Do you normally trust others?
- Do you blurt out whatever that comes to you?
- Do you think about what you are going to speak?
- Do you worry about things often?
- Are you discouraged easily?
- Do you normally complete the tasks assigned to you?
- Do you get angry easily?
- Do you use others for your own end?
- Do you tidy up your place and get everything organized?
- Do you often feel sad?
- Do you control any situation and take charge of it?
- Do you love to help others?
- Do you keep your promises?
- Are you always purposefully engaged?
- Do you love excitement?
- Do you love to read and get updated on what is happening around?
- Do you panic easily?
- Do you jump into things without thinking?
- Do you radiate joy?
- Do you challenge authority?
- Do you sympathize with the homeless and orphans?
- Do you believe others have good intentions?
- Do you get irritated easily?
- Do you cheat to get ahead?
- Do you like to put things back in their places?
- Do you dislike yourself?
- Do you try to lead others?
- Are you concerned about others?
- Do you always tell the truth?
- Do you work more than expected of you?
- Are you capable of using computers for proper communication and knowledge?
- Are you polite and friendly while using mobiles?
- Do you overindulge in drinking and eating?

- Do you seek adventure?
- Do you think highly of yourself?
- Do you get overwhelmed by events?
- Do you have a lot of fun in your life?
- Do you love debates and intellectual discussions?
- Are you humorous?
- Are you an achiever? Are you a person who is internally motivated and continuously driven for achievement?
- Do you care most about others and how they treat you?
- Do you wish to exercise power and authority over others?

After going through this questionnaire and answering them honestly you may decide the type of person you are: emotional, confident, self-centred, social, ambitious, charismatic, leader, follower, thinker, doer, giver, outgoing, extrovert, introvert, tidy and organized, honest and so on. Ascertain your positive and negative sides. Make a list of your drawbacks which you need to change or correct.

Chapter-4

Become ambitious

"Intelligence without ambition is a bird without wings."

—Salvador Dali

> *"Ambition can be defined as a strong desire for success of any goal through hard work and determination. The great achievers of the world possess this quality. Ambitious individuals constantly strive towards their goals and dreams."*

Even developing your personality requires ambition and striving. You can achieve nothing without some dreaming and real sweat.

Ambition is an important personality trait that helps us to usher in positive life outcomes. It is a path to success. It impacts our behaviour more directly than many other traits. Ambitious people have an enduring interest in seeing their efforts produce successful outcomes. They value doing their job well to climb up in their chosen field.

A team of leading organizational psychology researchers has shown through their extensive research that ambition has positive long term implications in life. One's persistent and generalized striving for success, attainment, and accomplishment are really critical to succeed.

We all know that nothing can be achieved with ease and leisure. You require dreams, hard work, persistence and focus. As Helen Keller said, "Character cannot be developed in ease and quiet. Only through experience of trial and suffering can the soul be strengthened, ambition inspired, and success achieved." Big results require big ambition and big efforts.

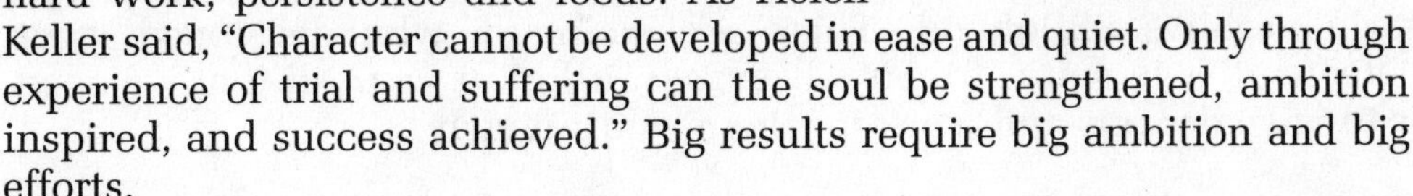

If you are ambitious you will propel yourself for success in education, profession, social life, health and longevity. It does not constitute a character flaw which leads to the dishonesty and dissatisfaction as alleged by critics throughout the ages. All agree that the habitual level of striving for or desiring accomplishment in life situations is highly positive and desirable.

There are people who credit their success to their hard work. Ambitious people are willing to work more and go the extra mile in order to achieve their goals. This seems to be the main difference between those who succeed and those who don't.

All these do not mean having more fun in life or enjoying family life is all that undesirable. There are different sets of values followed by different individuals.

- But you can be ambitious to develop a good personality so that you are successful in anything you choose. Your real ambition can be to become a complete pleasant, positive human being who is welcomed anywhere.

Why are some people very ambitious and others not? It greatly depends on how hard parents push their children to succeed, and what is the parent's expectation of the child. The more ambitious ones may have parents grooming them from an early age to succeed, while the parents of the non-ambitious may not care. By this, don't think that parental grooming is a pre-requisite to become ambitious. We all are ambitious in some sense and we can make our ambitions stronger as we grow.

Why do we desire to develop our personality? Probably, to become successful. Ambitious individuals will fight towards their goals regardless of the circumstances, adversities or setbacks. There is no alibi for not being ambitious. Your home-environment might not have been all that good, your physique, IQ –level may not be all that great too. But there is nothing that stops you from being ambitious.

Stop feeling bad about yourself

Who wants to know your history? There might be some negativity in your personality ingrained or inherited from your early childhood or your parents. The only relevant question will be: have you succeeded? There are enough endowments in you to make yourself successful and develop a good personality and don't lie down licking your wounds.

Positive philosophers stress that we make what we are and that we are totally free to grow and develop. Your personality development might have been adversely affected by your parents, home environment and early negative childhood. There are so many who developed great personalities in spite of their adversities. **All of us can. All that we need is to have dreams and work for them continuously**.

Some are lazy by nature

Instead of being ambitious and working hard to achieve goals, many people tend to do what is just required to earn a living and survive. They then spend the rest of their time enjoying and entertaining themselves.

The end result is that they remain in the same situation throughout their lives.

Successful people do not go after immediate pleasure gratification but work hard for later enjoyment. A person who prefers to watch TV now than work is seeking immediate gratification. You must be willing to put up with a certain amount of discomfort now for the attainment of something much better later. Successful individuals learn the personality characteristics of success and failure and spend the majority of their time doing the things that would bring success into their lives and avoid the things that won't. It is not all that easy and it may be hard and you may feel dispirited as you keep working. Majority of us are unwilling to choose the harder line and that is why more of us are failures in life.

Given a choice would you work hard or spend time with friends or simply play and have fun? Most of us will choose the latter. Most of the things which are fun and easy rarely bring success into our lives. But that is what we tend to do. After work we come home and relax spending time in front of the TV or computer. Ambitious and successful people fight the urge to choose between what is easy and fun.

But certain ambitions can be counter-productive. Trying to know everything about a celebrity or a sports team may help him/her boast to his friends about his expert knowledge but it will not be of any help to him in his life unless he pursues that career.

Ambition is the fuel that keeps us going good. Without it, we will wander without direction. A life without purpose can stagnate and can sometimes be a little boring. To be ambitious doesn't necessarily mean that you need to set high goals like becoming famous or winning Nobel Prize. Try to set your sights on an objective that stretches your potential a little, encourages you to become a better person, and gives you a sense of pride when you think of accomplishing it. You can also strive to be a better parent, groom and dress well always, practise healthy habits, learn new skills, be more organized, lose weight, or quit smoking.

Let's have concern for others too

There is no point in trying to achieve everything for ourselves. Having all the material possessions may not make us really happy or contended. We must strive to help others, wipe their tears and try to make our fellow beings happier and more comfortable. **As Cesar Chavez said,** *"We cannot seek achievement for ourselves and forget about progress and prosperity for our community... Our ambitions must be broad enough to include the aspirations and needs of others, for their sakes and for our own."*

We must strive to make our world a little better for all. As Jim Henson has said, "When I was young, my ambition was to be one of the people who made a difference in this world. My hope is to leave the world a little better for having been there."

❖❖

Chapter-5

Have an aim in life

"The future belongs to those who believe in the beauty of their dreams."

—Eleanor Roosevelt

*I*f you don't know where you are going you will never reach anywhere. Most of your energy and efforts will not be streamlined or it will get simply dissipated on your wayside. You will be a slave of your circumstances and other people's. Your progress or development will totally depend on your luck. You will rarely be able to make things happen. To change all these, set an aim for your life. One can have several aims; but choose a chief one to make good progress.

Having a goal and a plan to reach there at an early age has a big impact on life. It can better your personality, finances, improve relationships and further your career. Those who fail do not make strategies.

A study on 1979 Harvard MBA students revealed that only 3% of the graduates had written goal and plans. 13% had not-written goals and 84% had no specific goal at all. It was found, 10 years later, that the 13% of the class having a goal were earning, on an average, twice as much as the 84% who had no goals. And the 3% who had clear written goals, were earning 10 times as much as the 97% put together.

Where am I now and where do I want to reach? How do I get there? Can you list down the benefits you will get by reaching there? It is a good way to start planning now without worrying about what is going to happen. Identify your aim, plan and chart out a course. A well-thought out plan should give you a concrete time-table and clearly defined steps to reach your objectives with deadlines. You will need to develop the skills too for each one of the objectives in mind.

When you have a destination with a route-map, actions and strategies to reach there, your personality will automatically get better and charismatic; you will be driven with a purpose. You follow your star and you have no time to indulge in nonsenses or waste it away. Being on the go instills drive and confidence, two essential traits of a good personality. If you have no aim in life and float like a log of wood, you will wander here and there, stoop your shoulders and feel bad about yourself undermining your self-esteem. Ambition carries you forward making you hold your head aloft and always assume a confident posture.

As **Collin Powell** said, *"A dream doesn't become reality through magic; it takes sweat, determination and hard work."*

Finding out your purpose of life

Michael Gerber's book, The E-Myth poses the question, "What is your primary aim in life?" He asks, "With no clear picture of how you wish your life to be, how on earth can you begin to live it?"

In his book, *Blue Zones* Dan Buettner points out that when a person has a clear sense of purpose in his life, he will statistically live longer and have better health.

Questions helping you in setting a goal

- What should I become in my life and how should my life be like?
- How would I like to be with other people in my life–my family, friends and colleagues?
- How would I like people to think about me?
- What would I like to be doing say, 5 years from now? Twenty years from now?
- What specifically would I like to learn during my life?
- What is my primary aim in life?

Purposes applicable to all of us

- You need to live with purpose and passion every day;
- Be a great husband/wife, father/mother/son/daughter and foster meaningful relationships with friends and family;
- You can try to be financially sound;
- You can aim to be healthy, active and fit;
- Always try to be learning, never give up, and give my best each day;
- Help others in all the above.

All of us have some goals and dreams. But some of us seem to be more successful at achieving them than others. Why? Natural talent? The right connections? Just plain dumb luck? Sometimes those reasons are correct, but more often, people who achieve their goals are those who chose the right goals in the right time and follow them steadfastly.

If we really want to be successful in life, we have to choose the goals that are right for us. We are all unique and our goals should reflect that. If you want success in life, you need to choose goals that are congruent with your values, your strengths, your passions and your desired lifestyle. It goes without saying that you need to know what is your natural bend of mind, your talents and what you enjoy doing. In other words, choose goals that are congruent with your person, likings, dislikings, natural talent and aspirations.

So how do you choose? What do you need to make sure that your goals suite you and that they will guarantee your success? You need to ask yourself some questions:

What do you love most?

- money;
- power;
- friendship;
- family;
- public life;
- helping others;
- professional success.

Questions relevant in choosing aims in life

- When have you been happiest in your life?
- What has made you truly proud of yourself?
- What qualities do you admire most in other people?
- What makes you feel really alive and energized?
- If you had just 1 year to live, how would you spend it?
- If you could change one thing about the world, what would it be?
- What will make your life happier?

What are my strengths?

Enumerate each one of them:

- General/specialized knowledge;
- Ability to draw/paint/sing/act/speak/repair/write;
- Meeting people and pleasing them;

- Good IQ and memory;
- Pleasing appearance and politeness;
- Focus and concentration;
- Willingness to work hard;
- Willingness to help others and so on.

If you are having difficulty assessing yourself, or if you'd like a second opinion, ask your bosom friends what they think your strengths are. They may offer some insight that you never imagined as strength of yours.

What do I love doing?

Unless we know the answer to this question we will choose something that is not inherently suited to us and will live unhappy most of the time.

Write down the things that you enjoy spending time with. They can be related to your work or your personal life. These should be things that make you happy, that you really enjoy doing.

Sometimes we get so lost in what we are doing and we lose track of time. This happens when we are doing something we love. Taking a little trip back in time can help us to uncover passions that we have ignored. It can be anything like singing, writing, drawing or painting, fixing things up, directing, acting try to identify what you enjoy most. Choose your goal in what you enjoy best.

Your goals must be achievable and should match your nature, what you love doing, your emotional level and capabilities. If you are not sure where you're going or if you don't know what you want to achieve in life, give yourself time to think. Look deep inside. Try to know yourself more and then choose your goals.

If you do not feel fulfilled or happy with your life now, you may evaluate your life and the work you do. You may have been living your life the wrong way. It is never too late to change or make changes in your life-style and work and start living a life that is meaningful and happy. Find your life's purpose and then take action to implement the kind of life you really want to live.

You can have more than one purpose

Many people think that their purpose has to revolve around one thing. Sometimes you will have to balance different aspects of your needs and wants. Sometimes, one purpose can be made up of multiple facets offering you more flexibility.

Let us suppose your life's purpose is to become happy and make others happy. You can have the sub-purpose: to go the extra mile in your job so that you feel fulfilled and happy. You can try to be nice and patient with your family. You can spend more time with your children, listen more to people with problems and so on.

Make necessary changes in your goal as you move on and avoid actions that will detract you from it. Once you have written down your goal make it your personal life mission, carry it each minute in your mind, meditate upon it, believe you will achieve it and work hard for it focusing your mental and physical energies. There is no need to try to please.

Can you aspire to become a great personality?

Possible. But all of us can't become Lincoln, Einstein, Picasso, or Shakespeare. You must have heard, 'aim high; sky is your limit.' But in practical terms we have our own limitations and limits. Our IQ, EQ, structure of brain, our biology, childhood environment, parents and experiences of developmental stages have set limits on us. But we can aspire to go higher in our innate field and flower our talents. And anyone can try to be happy and develop a pleasant, likeable personality welcomad anywhere.

Chapter-6

Comprehensive worldview

"There are more things in heaven and earth, Horatio, than are dreamt of in your philosophy."

—Shakespeare, Hamlet

A worldview is a theory of the world, used for living in the world. A world view is a mental model of reality — a framework of ideas and attitudes about the world, ourselves, and life — a comprehensive system of beliefs.

Worldview is just a term meaning how you interpret reality, life, after-life, gods, ethics morals, earth, solar system, galaxies and the universe. We are vastly influenced by the thoughts and beliefs of those we read, watch or associate with. We slowly develop a unique perspective on what is going on. In general, our worldview has been most influenced by home, religion and science.

Some world view questions are about the supernatural. Do they exist or are they created by religions? Isn't the universe self-creating? Is not life just a long string of things happening? What happens after death?

One cannot be confined to one's religion, beliefs or culture to the exclusion of all others. Develop a world view about the universe, how life developed here and where it is going. Know what is going on in the world. **Nobody is impressed with a person** who doesn't even know what is happening around or in the world. No wise man or woman would like to befriend or follow him. There are so many ways to better your comprehensive world view: read good books, watch informative programmes and interact or interrelate with intelligent persons.

We live on a minor planet of an average star located in the outer limits of the Milky Way galaxy which contains over 200 billion stars. All the planets with their satellites revolve round the sun which in turn, along with all of them goes round the galactic nucleus at a very high speed.

There are over one hundred thousand million galaxies in the universe! Scientists think there are a greater number of such universes! Against these scales, even our Milky Way galaxy, (dia.100,000 light years) wherein our own sun is just an ordinary star is just a speck or a dot; our sun a negligible object and the earth infinitesimal.

In an earth-like planet with the optimum gravity to retain an atmosphere, at an optimum distance from the sun (to get just enough energy) with an abundance of elements, life evolved through random chemical reactions and later, through evolution, reached the levels of an advanced civilization we see today. There can be millions of earth-like planets in the universe with life in many of them. Due to the huge distances involved, we do not know each other. The entire solar system and the life on planet earth will end with the death of our sun in a supernova after about 4 billion years.

Thousands of billions of people have taken birth here and gone. A majority of them died before they reached the age of ten or less. Billions have perished in natural calamities and an equal number in wars fought for gods, religions, powerful guys and nations. No one over 125 years is alive today. That is our maximum life-span. But this small planet has been there, almost in the same form, for the last 4200000000 years! It may be there for another 40000000000 years! But we humans are like an air bubble, forming and bursting out almost simultaneously.

Man evolved from the lower mammals like chimpanzees probably in Africa and later spread out to the different continents. Geography and climate made him black, white, yellow coloured with myriad physical, linguistic and cultural differences. Temperate areas advanced more than the hot climate ones; regions like America, northern Europe, Japan, South Korea, Singapore, Australia and New Zealand are all rich and prosperous. Sub Saharan Africa and Sothern Asia are poor and underdeveloped. Ethnic, nationalistic, linguistic and religious differences have brought about innumerable conflicts.

Man's life had been extremely difficult in the early years. Food was scarce and he had to face the fury of nature, diseases and death. But his powerful procreative faculties made him survive and proliferate. He tamed animals, discovered agriculture, developed industry and started to make his life comfortable in the recent past.

During the early stages of human evolution he was awe struck at the wonderful nature-phenomena. Many of them like the sun and moon were good and he started making them benevolent gods (deification of nature-phenomena).The forces which caused floods, hurricanes, thunder and lightening, earthquakes, volcanic eruptions, contagious diseases and plagues became evil gods. He started pleasing the former and appeasing the latter.

Further he was puzzled at the death of a friend who was walking with him just the other day. Something must have left his corpse (the body remains intact after death-at least for a small period) and naturally he started thinking of a spirit that must have left the corpse. This is the beginning of animism –the cult of the spirits. Man was sad of his mortality and he longed to live eternally like the gods he made. All these together laid the foundations for the various religions we see today. Millions of gods of all shapes and hues got evolved and some of them became superior to the others. Later, in tandem with the rise of powerful kings and emperors, the concept of a supreme god evolved too. Religious leaders of different natures established different ways to live here to please his gods. Buddha, Confucius, Christ, Muhammad all had their own versions.

The discovery of agriculture and evolution of human societies made religions organized too. Today, we have atheistic Buddhism, Adwaithic Hinduism, Monotheistic Christianity, Judaism and Islam, Atheistic Communism, and a large number of animistic beliefs. There are hundreds of warring sects for each one of the major religions. Religions have caused thousands of wars, communal strife and they have harmed the peaceful co-existence of man.

Parents programme children to believe their religion

The brain washing is so intense and deep rooted that normally they come to believe their religion is the only true one. Perhaps it is interesting to note that these religions are fundamentally different in the concept of their gods, how man should live here and eve the nature of an afterlife. Even the ultimate purpose of life varies totally from one to the other. For the Hindus it is cessation from the chain of birth and rebirth, for the Buddhists it is Nirvana or total detachment, for the Muslims it is a material heaven where every conceivable pleasure is available and the Christians speak of a spiritual life with the godhead. Even today, in the midst of an advanced civilization, almost half of all men still believe in a religion of some sort–more due to the force of habit and early childhood programmeming than due to any other cause.

We have these enigmatic 100 odd years in front of us. We can live it in the delusion of a god, heaven and do everything for the afterlife. Or, we can understand the true facts of life and face things squarely living this life happily and successfully with a lot of celebration, helping fellow beings and at last go with a gratitude that we got a chance to come down here.

Chapter-7

Become positive

We all concentrate on the cons first, are reluctant to spare a compliment and do not even broadcast a smile. What's more, we prefer to criticize, find fault and pass sarcastic comments. Deep down we all seem to believe the glass is actually half empty. We live in negativity all the time and lament the world around is mean and hostile. At the work place we always tell all concerned how tough things are and the difficulties one is to confront ahead.

Unlike dogs, we are not born optimists, but positivity is something that can be imbibed with a little effort. We can try to see the brighter side of things, see the good things in others, and tweak our sense of humour a little. We can with practise change the way we react to a given bad situation internally and externally. We can start believing the world and others are good and we can endeavour to be consciously pleasant and smile each time we meet someone.

THINK POSITIVE, & POSITIVE THINGS WILL HAPPEN

The way we think has a lot of effect on the way we act. Positive thoughts give one confidence to boost and enhance his personality. Situations and circumstances in life will always have highs and lows. In order to adopt a positive outlook towards life, you need to develop the habit of finding the brighter sides of the things and focus on the good sides of anything.

The world is not against you and **no one is born with a 'grey cloud' over his head. The Universe wants you to succeed and become happy.** You can easily overcome the ordeals of childhood; the pain, failures and disappointments of the past need not repeat in your future endeavours.

Do not let a self-fulfilling prophecy to work in your life. (If you expect bad results there is a higher likelihood that they happen.) Do not worry about what is happening to you and what has happened to you so far, but think about what you can make happen. Learn from the past and set new goals (be careful in their choice–you should simply enjoy working for them) and pursue them.

One of the very first things you have to start to work on consciously with your personal development is to improve your outlook on life. If you continue looking at the positive sides of life for a few years, a stable attitude would develop over time and you would start seeing only the positive sides of events and experiences, people and events in your life. You could turn positive and constructive even during tough times and keep working towards something better.

Mantras to become positive

1. Clinical psychologists feel that to become a positive person **one must have a strong desire to be positive.** And the desire will come only if you are convinced that becoming a positive person will enhance the quality of life. Becoming a positive person does not mean you will never have any negative emotion or situation. It is the attitude that matters. We don't have to get bogged down by failure, and disappointed when expectations are not met.
2. When you have failed or made a mistake-instead of cursing or telling yourself, it's my fate, you ask yourself: **What is one positive or good thing about this situation?** Is there an opportunity hidden within this? Don't try to force such a question right away. Let your sad feelings run through its course. Trying to force optimistic thinking when you are still feeling bad or a bit depressed usually doesn't work well.
3. *It's essential to keep away from negative people who discourage you or who point out other failures and drag you still deeper into an emotional turmoil.* Identify at least 2 negative people whom you spend time with. Find out 2 sources that feed negative information too. Any party that blames your circumstance, society for your ills is such a source. Even a TV programme with this message is harmful. Positivity and negativity are infectious. If the people you spend most of your time with are grumpy or have a pessimistic standpoint, you'll find yourself mirroring the same emotions.
4. To be able to stay positive it is essential to have influences in your life that support you and lift you up instead of dragging you down. *Have ambitious and successful people as your bosom friends.* Read self-help books on personal achievement. Get inspired from the lives of those who rose up in spite of severe handicaps.
5. At times of crisis, don't be too fast, think in steps. Walk, talk and eat slower to make yourself calmer. It becomes easier that way to think things through clearly and to find an optimistic and constructive perspective.
6. **Daily meditation** will calm your nerves down and help you think in a more peaceful way to analyze things more constructively. You may sit relaxed, close your eyes, take a few deep slow breaths and count from ten to bring a panoramic location to your mind, and keep void for a few

minutes. Alternately, you may run through the confident experiences of your life. *It's good to learn yoga and Pranayama and practise it on a daily basis.* These produce a surge of positive energy through your body that calms your nerves, soothes your mind, elevates your mood, and your level of tolerance. (You may read more on the chapter on meditation.)

7. **Don't blow up your present problem.** Sometimes people make a mountain out of a molehill. When failure happens or challenge presents itself, you have the habit of making it disproportionately huge. You relate your problem to someone you can trust and you may get a better perspective. My wife has been cooling me down for years whenever a challenge presents itself. Sometimes she just brushes it aside and at other times she shows me its impact is minimal. Then if there is a real problem she is there to face it with me.
8. When you want to do a new project why should you get lost in vague fears about what could happen if you go ahead. Spend a bit of time trying to figure out what you could do if the worst thing, pretty unlikely, happens. *Remember more than 90% of all worries never happen.*
9. Help others, listen to those who have problems and boost people's mood. What you think about people, what you give and how you treat them is what you'll get back. *When you think good, do good and treat them good you think and treat yourself better.*
10. Exercise regularly, eat and sleep well. Being careful about these basic habits may sound boring. But they do have a huge effect on your positivity.
11. One of the most common fears is the fear of criticism. It can hold people back from doing what they want in life. But if you want to take action on what you want to do then criticism is pretty much unavoidable. Let them criticize. You go the way you feel correct and fit and take the good points from each criticism you hear.
12. *Start your day in a positive way.* How you start your day usually sets the tone for the rest of your day. Wake up from bed energetically, think about all the good points of yesterday, have a nice word to your family and move on with hope and energy.
13. Concentrate on the present task and don't dwell on your past or future and worry. Don't allow the failures and mistakes from the past to get replayed over and over in your mind dragging you down into pessimism. Let the past bury the past. Simply ask your mind to shut it off and concentrate on the present and future.
14. Make a list of your positive qualities and achievements and post them where you can see them very often. Recall moments from your past life when you felt confident, happy and winner. Recall events when you stood up to your father, principal or any superior. Simply list

down experiences when you felt you were on the top of the world. Go through them occasionally seeing in your mind's eyes what you had seen brightly and in colour, magnifying every sound you had heard and experience every feeling you had experienced more intensely.

15. **Start savouring everything good life has to offer.** More money need not necessarily make you happier. You have so much to be happy about: your dear ones, your friends and your children, your day-to-day life with them, and your small achievements. Emphasize your pluses and down play your shortcomings.
16. **Make sure you enjoy your work.** If it is boring or creating tension in you try to find out another one that you can enjoy. There are people who simply ignore this suggestion and trundle on unhappy and miserable. We have only one life, why do we have to torment ourselves? Quitting and finding a new work may not be easy. But it is worth the effort. Getting over difficulties is how we live and progress.
17. **Forgive everyone who has harmed you before.** Forgiveness has a great positive impact on your happiness. Do not torment yourself with grudge or enmity.
18. When something goes wrong, try to figure it out and fix it up; do not indulge in self-pity or curse your fate.
19. Taking care to **dress smartly** each day helps to have a sunny feeling. Try and make positive words a part of your daily life let your erect confident body language show you are friendly and approachable.
20. ***Always try to do more than you are expected of****–instead of doing just enough to pull on with your job. It will increase your self-esteem and confidence.*
21. The ambitious ones work harder and longer with fewer breaks. Are you always busy and still achieve nothing? Do you miss those beautiful and joyous moments of life simply because you're always caught up with one thing or another? Many feel it is good to take a little time off to look into yourself to see what is going on in your life, to examine your work, health, relationships, just to take some time to be with your inner self. Moments of silence could be found anytime during a day to reflect on the good things that happen in life and to feel grateful to nature and the people around you.
22. ***Do not remain idle and brood.*** Take up positive activities with others: share a joke, go out with friends, take part in sporting activities, go for a run in the evening after work, have healthy sex, and you'll find yourself bubbling with positive energy.
23. **Maintain a good-luck diary.** Filter out the positive events of each day and make a note of them. It could be anything trivial from your bus arriving on time, having a delicious breakfast, getting back a debt, helping a poor man, someone's good words to you, boss behaving nicely, getting your task finished on time or any such thing. When

we focus on positive things there will be no room for negativity. Read through the list before you sleep and savour the good things of that day.

You need to follow a set of positive values in your life. Each company expects an employee to be

- Honest;
- Ethical;
- Just and fair;
- Respectful of others;
- Complying with its policies, procedures and rules;
- Hardworking with initiative;
- Aware of the company's aims and objectives and strive for them;
- A team player and co-operative with others.

Each one of you needs to keep these in mind when you try developing a positive personality.

Negatives and positives always come mixed– that's the way life is. Just like an optimist says the glass is half full and not half empty, you may concentrate on the good things. Focusing on the bad will only make you sadder. There will be nine pluses for each minus point in your life. But the problem is that we all concentrate only on the negatives always and seldom look at the ample good things around. Being optimistic does not mean you are ignoring or denying your problems. And thinking positive does not insure one against failure. They will come and we have to prepare ourselves to meet them squarely. You may 'hope for the best but prepare for the worst.'

Chapter-8

Always be yourself

"To be yourself in a world that is constantly trying to make you something else is the greatest accomplishment."

—Ralph Waldo Emerson

You might have heard: just be yourself. What does it mean? You have to become your natural and real true self without masks and pretentions, after shredding to the floor whatever stuff other people have clothed you with. Each individual is different and unique with his own sets of skills and flaws. You cannot be another person. There are many who try to imitate other successful guys and fail miserably. Though you can always look up to the great or successful people to take an inspiration from, you should always remain your own unique self. Trying to be somebody else gets you nowhere and it simply backfires. You can try to fit in or belong to a new group without shedding your authenticity and individuality. Never try moulding into another person but try to work on being the best version of yourself.

Become like kids

Children are totally free to be what they are and who do not care about what other people think of them. They are happy the way they are. They do what comes naturally to them. People may think they are silly as they dance in the front yard for all of the neighbours to see. Children are just pure love and light. If you really want to get in touch with your inner child, become free, play, have fun, enjoy the moment, do what you innately want.

We are often stiff and serious. We put on masks to hide our true natures. We play roles to fit into society and we suppress our true nature out of fear of what others will think.

Never lose a chance to project your true self. If you are in a group or talking with an individual you must talk and behave in a way that your inner self is truly projected always. Become true to yourself.

Can you find out what you are? Can you identify your values and take time to consider what makes up the essence of you. Think about your life and its choices. What kind of things you would and you wouldn't like to do? Look deep inside yourself and think about who you are. Once you know yourself then it's easier to become yourself and act as you. Trying to mimic or model another person won't help at all. You are yourself and give expression to yourself politely but unassumingly.

Listen to what Fyodour Dostoyevsky has to say: "To go wrong in one's own way is better than to go right in someone else's."

You have your own style, your own ways of expressing and your own mannerisms and your own ways of responding. If they produce positive outcomes, good. If you are resented, you will have to correct yourself perhaps following the suggestions of a well-wisher whom you trust. You will have a unique way of communicating and behaving. You can't be like a billionaire or a celebrity. By comparing with others, never try to belittle yourself. Whatever be the style of famous people or local hero you have your own style and be happy about it. Don't beat yourself at any cost.

You will have your own values, opinions, beliefs and your own ways of behaviour. It isn't necessary to change them to please others. Just keep in mind people love those who are likeable, unpretentious, flexible and easy going. Hence, stop adapting yourself to other people's expectations. Whatever you are, accept it. Being different is absolutely beautiful and it attracts people to you. **People admire a person of integrity than the one who keeps changing.**

But in the garb of asserting yourself, you cannot be rude or impolite. If so, you have to correct yourself. If you don't follow etiquette and good manners you won't be accepted by anyone and you will be generally unwelcomed in any group.

- Be honest and open. What have you got to hide? We're all imperfect–growing and learning human beings. If you feel ashamed or insecure about any aspect of yourself and you feel that you have to hide those parts of you, you have to come to terms with that and acknowledge them as your imperfections.
- Suppose there is an argument with your room-mate regarding you messing up the common room. Own upto your shortcoming is a matter-of-factway. The moment you say, "look, we all get really irritable when the room's in a mess. I shouldn't leave my clothes in a pile on the floor and yet I do it because I'm lazy. I'm trying to come out of the habit. I'm sorry." You suddenly infuse an argument with genuine self-honesty that disarms the entire point of the argument.

Don't compare yourself to others. If you're striving to be someone else, you'll never be a happy person. This happens when you compare yourself to others and find out that you lack some desirable qualities or ways. This will lead you to feel inferior, insecure and make you become more negative. By comparing yourself to others, you give their image-portrayal too much power and reduce your own worth. It's a useless activity that only brings harm. Value the person you are, love your personality, and embrace your flaws; we all have them, and as explained earlier, being honest is better than running away from what you are.

Maybe we can keep in mind what Oliver James said: "Do your own thing on your own terms and get what you came here for."

Stop bothering about how people see or perceive you. Some of them will like you and some of them won't. Either attitude is likely to be right or wrong.

- Do they think I'm stupid?
- Does he think I'm fat?
- Do they think I'm funny?
- Am I good or clever enough to be a part of their group?
- Am I old-fashioned?
- Do I measure up to their modern ways?

Forget about what others think about you and let your behaviour flow, with consideration and politeness for others. It's difficult to be yourself when you're caught up constantly wondering how others will see you. If you change yourself for one person or group, that change may not be appreciated by another person or group and you could go on in a vicious cycle trying to please others instead of focusing on building up your strengths.

Stop pleasing others. There are those who always want everyone's love and respect. It's a futile wish and your related attempts are meaningless. Sometimes these acts may harm your personality development and confidence. You shouldn't care what other people say unless they are well-meaning people who are genuinely interested in your development.

Follow Eleanor Roosevelt's advice: "No one can make you feel inferior without your consent and what matters most is that you listen to your own inner confidence and if it's missing, then you start developing it!"

We don't mean to say that others' opinions don't matter. They do. Of course it hurts if you're a social outcast, if you have to spend all of your time among people who can't stand you. Maybe you can pay attention to people who genuinely desire your well-being and who want you to achieve your goals in life.

Accept healthy criticism; dismiss pointless, sarcastic or negative comments. Listen to what parents, mentors, teachers, coaches, might be telling you; you need to digest and think over what they mention at your own pace and make self-improvements. They care about you and they criticize you to help you grow well.

Be considerate to yourself. Treat yourself kindly and respectfully as you treat other people you care about. Tell yourself you're confident, special, wonderful, and worthwhile and make honest attempts to become so. When you believe these things about yourself, others will recognize that glow of self-confidence and begin confirming to your self-affirmations in no time! If you lack self-esteem and self-worth feelings, others may not respect or welcome you for long. You will get a lot of tips as to how to develop positive qualities as you read on.

Each day is not all that fun. On some days people might try to make fun of you. Stand your ground and say, hey, ' that's the way I am.' They will ultimately respect you for what you are. Sometimes it may hurt when you are teased. This can be very difficult, and it is easier said than practised—try to ignore it or flick it off your shoulder. After some time they will accept you as a better person, and you will be able to survive whatever obstacles arise in your future. If, on the other hand, you resent or fight with them, you alone will stand to lose.

Avoid being rude, thoughtless and egoistic to others. Respect them as much as you respect yourself. Please don't ram your views and opinions down other people's throats! Everyone has points of views and beliefs that are equally deserving and it's up to each one of us to acknowledge the others' values as much as our own.

Ignore what other people will think of it. This is perhaps the most important aspect in being you. As mentioned, your life and happiness cannot depend on what others may think or say. Let us concentrate on our happiness and not on others. Don't suppress your inner self to please others or to simply fit in.

You might have taken a course of study for others, you may have moved to the city to please your people and you may have stayed in an unhappy job fearing what others may think or say. Try to become you. Live your life in alignment with your inner soul. Change your job if it is miserable and doesn't make you happy. Follow your inner urges even in little things like the way you dress, combing your hair or grooming your moustache and beard.

Find something you like and can do well, try to do it over and over. If you spend your time doing things you're not good at, it'll frustrate you and cause you to feel defeated and unsuccessful.

Get rid of your conditioned negative thoughts

There are a number of negative thoughts that run through your mind each day and we try to conform to these thoughts and our reality becomes accordingly. We have many unconscious beliefs that were probably handed down to us from somebody else which we believe to be true. Become more aware of your thoughts, let go off the old beliefs, and become more present so that you can reveal your true nature.

Never say negative things about you—

- "I never do anything right."
- "I'll never change."
- "I'm ugly."
- "I look terrible."
- "I'm dumb."
- "Who could ever love me?"

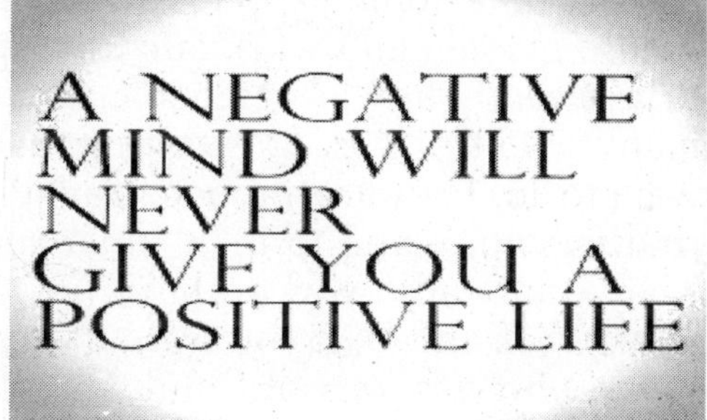

The way we talk and think about ourselves reveals how we feel about ourselves. Change your negative self-talks and make them positive thus:

- "I am OK."
- "I'll accomplish that."
- "I can change."
- "I have done a number of things right."

Simply start thinking and speaking good things about yourself. Focus on your potential instead of your limitations.

Napoleon Bonaparte, Lal Bahadur Shasthri were all short people. But they were tall to others. Helen keller was blind, deaf and mute but she made so many others see and hear. Sometimes your shortfall can be a blessing in disguise if you focus on your strengths. List down all your inner abilities and try to tap them.

The most important thing we can do to become our true self is to pursue the goals that are right for us. If we choose wrong ones, if we pursue goals that are not in conformity with what we are, what we care about, and what we like, then even if we achieve those goals, we are not going to feel happy or fulfilled.

- Do not jump into action on dreaming or thinking about anything; take time to pay attention to how you feel about it. Scientists believe that people who are mindful in this way are more likely to pursue goals that are consistent with whom they really are.

Are you surrounded by people who make it easy to be your true self?

The people around you can be important in making it easier for you to become your best self.

- You will do well in the workplace if you have a boss who tries to see your perspective and who tries to provide meaningful rationales for any advice that is offered.
- Having a supportive coach can be especially important for any athlete.

Some of us are fortunate to have friends or relatives who know us better than we know ourselves, and have our best interests in mind. They might know a goal we are going to pursue may never make us happy. They will know how to tell us that in a way we will listen too.

Society and home people always tell us to find a steady job, a safe and secure income and work our way up. They feel that it is easy for anyone to succeed in any job. Hence many of us just find a job to go on. But later many who feel they are wasting their time, doing things that they do not want to do. They are trapped in an unhappy, unfulfilled existence–without finding expression to their inner self and their own special uniqueness. They frantically work to have fun on the weekends, and then loath the work week ahead. If you want to live an extraordinary life you better first know who you truly are, and what your inner strengths are and what you want in life.

"Waking up to who you are requires letting go off who you imagine yourself to be." Alan Watts.

Let us conclude the thoughts on 'Always try to be yourself,' by quoting what Victoria Moran says:

"If you celebrate your differentness, the world will, too. It believes exactly what you tell it—through the words you use to describe yourself, the actions you take to care for yourself and the choices you make to express yourself. Tell the world you are one-of-a-kind creation who came here to experience wonder and spread joy. Expect to be accommodated."

Chapter-9

Become a life-learner

"I do not think much of a man who is not wiser today than he was yesterday."

—Abraham Lincoln

A man of little knowledge or interests has very little to talk about. *But if you are well informed about things and cultivate a number of interests, more people tend to like you.* You can strike up interesting conversations instead of appearing to be dull and monotonous. When you meet new people you do not have to think about what to say as you can share your knowledge or your interests and get them indulged in conversations with you.

Learning should not stop with school or university. The world is changing every day, every hour with new discoveries, new approaches, new theories and tips. *People who are truly effective constantly learn to compete in the world and grow. Try to learn something new every day and apply your knowledge to become a better person, and to make the world a better place for you and for me.*

Information technology is at each one's doorstep and we all should access it and use this information for augmenting our knowledge. Our opinions must be supported by facts. And it is totally irresponsible to have loud and vociferous opinions on subjects one is ignorant about. The ability to form and articulate opinions is extremely important to have meaningful interaction with others. As citizens, we need to form opinions about political issues and leaders too. *Ultimately what you say makes you a more valuable or less valuable person.*

Having an opinion and being able to confidently put it forward helps your conversations to be more interesting and you look more influential and well informed around other people. Sometimes your opinions even may conflict with those of other people. *Dealing with healthy disagreements boosts your inner strength.* Hence try to be well informed about all the relevant stuff in your world by reading more, watching TV and acquiring knowledge through the net.

Learning things should not become a chore. Don't just force yourself to learn things because they're important or necessary. Instead, learn things that you need to learn alongside things you love to learn. Even when you're learning the things you have to, like the on-the-job knowledge, seek to go beyond and acquire adequate general knowledge to be welcomed in any group. *Reading is a portal into other worlds and into the minds of your fellow human beings. Sources are aplenty: newspapers, magazines, manuals, books, websites, blogs, reviews and other online sources of information. To make yourself a better person evaluate and reflect on what you read and learn.*

Social learning theory and personality development

People learn from one another through observation, modelling and imitation. You have to observe others' behaviour and attitudes. Most human learning is learnt observationally and through conscious or unconscious modelling. Infants learn to sit, stand, walk, run, talk and so on by observing and modelling their parents and close relatives. It has application in personality development too. *You can model the best dressed people with the best body language and communicative ability — political, public and business leaders — and develop better personalities.*

The most common examples of social learning situations are television commercials. Commercials suggest that using a particular hair shampoo will make us popular and win the admiration of attractive people. We may model the behaviour shown in the commercial and buy the product being advertised thinking and hoping we will also become like the models and win others' admiration.

But do the hair shampoo users get anything they imagined? No. Why? Because there is no co-relation between what the commercial made you feel and the reality. But people continue to buy the product as the modelling process is very often happening at the subconscious levels.

If you have observed **Barrack Obama,** you would certainly note that he carries himself erect, holding his head up with drawn shoulders. He is always well dressed and dignified. He is almost always in open with confident postures and gestures. He looks straight at the person or group he talks to and has a command of the language with correct diction and accent. His movements are brisk and he carries himself with dignity and briskness.

Researchers of the unit for the **Study of Personality in Politics, College of Saint Benedict, St. Joseph, MN 56374, U.S.A** have found Obama's primary personality patterns to be ambitious/confident, dominant/asserting, with secondary features of accommodating/cooperative and conscientious/respectful. The combination of ambitious and accommodating patterns in Obama's profile suggests a confident conciliator. He is a self-assured and assertive, gracious, charming, considerate, agreeable and benevolent leader with a strong need for affiliation.

Well we are not here interested in the theories of Obama's personality. But we are definitely concerned about how he carries himself, how he dresses and grooms and how he communicates. Well if you watch Obama, you will observe the following.

- He has erect posture.
- He is very fit, shapely and healthy.
- He holds his head aloft almost always with drawn shoulders.
- He normally looks straight (slightly upward).
- He has confident open gestures(his palm is almost always open, held in front going out of the body).
- He looks straight into the eyes of the other person or group.
- Look at him: A perfectly shaped individual who takes pain not to put on weight. He is so light and keeps his body mass index below the allowable limits. He looks perfectly fit, agile and flexible.

Obama's attire

- He is dressed smartly with a grey or bluish grey suite immaculately pressed and fitting him smugly.
- His tie is matching and beautiful, tied with a perfect knot.
- His shirt is normally white, again clean and well pressed.
- His shoes shine and are fresh and appropriate.

His body language and his attire together radiate confidence and assertiveness. Having been the US President, he carried tons of power too. But he used to be like this even before he became the president. Perhaps these qualities inculcated the enormous self-confidence that propelled him to the White House.

He was born of a black African father and a white mother and he inherited the African features but still he became the president of a white and most powerful nation. How he reached the most powerful position in the world? Certainly his body language, attire and communicative ability—his personality did help. And it is time we try to emulate him in these three major aspects.

- Take a decision today to adopt Obama's body language, fitness, dressing and grooming. Also make a decision to become an efficient communicator.
- Write it down in golden letters: I will always sit/stand/walk holding my head straight. I will always try to have open and confident postures and gestures. I will be immaculately dressed after cleaning myself thoroughly. There is no need to wear a suite or a tie all the time but dress smartly according to the Indian traditions and context.
- I will manicure and pedicure my fingers and toes. I will comb my hair, trim moustache/beard, and apply moisturizer on my skin and face.
- I will use modern branded clothes and I will take extra care to dress smartly. My footwear will be neat clean and elegant.
- I will adopt energized brisk movements. Walk briskly; sit erect, talk looking straight into the eyes of the other person and never stoop or walk clumsily dragging my feet or looking down.

I would like to mention here that you should love your dress. If you wear something you are not at ease with that is not going to help at all. Select whatever you love and you are happy about. But wear them immaculately and elegantly.

Obama had power in what he said. He has developed a powerful accent and pronunciation. His gestures are powerful too. You may not be doing a lot of public speeches. But you need to develop a commanding vocabulary, correct accent, pronunciation and diction. Since this book is in English, let us see how we can improve the language and its delivery. I will suggest a few points here to improve your English communication:

1. Watch and hear an English TV news programme for at least half an hour every day.
2. Write at least a page on any topic each day. This is not going to be easy and hence start writing on simple topics like 'my father', 'my mother', 'my village', ' my family' and so on.
3. Read English language newspaper before reading a vernacular one.
4. Mark the difficult words and phrases and try to use many of them in your daily scribbling.
5. You converse with someone in English at least for 5-10 minutes.

6. After you have practised these for over 3 months, try recording a talk of yours (after rehearsals) and play it back. Note the flaws in your accent, diction, pronunciation, use of phrases and appropriate words and take corrective steps.
7. Record again after a month. Continue this process until you feel confident with the language.

Any language can be developed in a similar way.

To carry out these things you need to have a strong desire to improve your personality and decide to carry the steps you have enumerated. If you practise the new body language ways for over one and half months without interruption they will become a habit of yours and you need not put any conscious effort any more to get the confident postures, brisk movements and better attire. They become part of your person; your inner make-up.

Chapter-10

Become fit

"Take care of your body. It's the only place you have to live."

—Jim Rohn

Our bodies are the temples of our souls. And most often these temples are ignored. If something is ignored it will cease to exist. Do you want to end your life?

See how you are in the mirror. Do you take sufficient care of it? What message does it give you? Are you physically fit? Are you careful in what you take in? Do you regularly exercise?

Whenever you eat something that your body finds hard to digest- fats, fried stuff and oily food- your body struggle to digest them. You are what you eat. *So closely monitor what goes in there.*

Whenever you hear music at high volume and pitch, whenever you see TV at close range, you are harming your organs. When you sit hunchbacked, you are harming your backbone. Posture, cleanliness is all quite important. When we bathe do we make sure to clean every part-including the back of your ears, webs of your toes, back of the knee, between your legs –to make sure every cell is neat? Take more time to bathe taking care of every single cell.

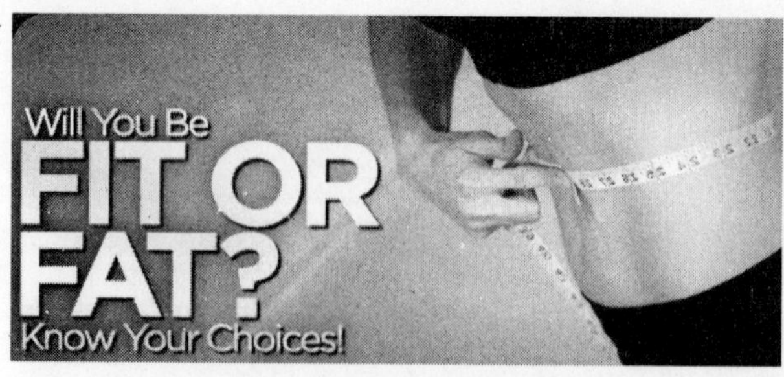

Fitness, in the simplest terms, is your ability to perform well in life. A fit person's personality is invariably better and he is more popular and more appreciated. It helps you to be efficient physically and mentally. A fit life is probably a lot more fun than a non-fit one. How do we know we are fit? Does absence of diseases make you fit? Being lean? The feeling I am alright? It can be none of these.

Some indicators are given below:

Your weight: If you are overweight you are obviously not fit. A thumb rule is to calculate your height in inches. That can be your weight in kilograms. If you are 5'10" it works out to 70 inches and ideal weight is 70 kilograms. You can use a formula given here under.

J. D. Robinson Formula (1983): 52 kg + 1.9 kg per inch over 5 feet (man)

49 kg + 1.7 kg per inch over 5 feet (woman).

BMI: Divide your weight in kilograms by the square of your height in metres. If your weight is 80kg, and height is 5 feet 10 inches (1.77M) your BMI is equal to 25.53(80 divided by 1.77x1.77) The World Health Organization (WHO) maintains BMI should be between 18.5 - 25 for both man and woman. In this instance you are overweight. To get to your ideal BMI, you should reduce your weight by about 10kgs.

Your waist line measurement is also an important indicator: Take a measure using a tape directly placed on your skin or on very light clothing halfway between your lowest rib and the top of your hip bone, breathing normally. Height does not affect much this measure. As per the WHO, if you more than 80cm (women) and 94cm (men) you are at an increased risk of some lifestyle related diseases and hence you are unfit.

Some other indicators are as follows:

1. Body-fat percentage— This is the per centage of your total body weight to the total fat weight in the body. 10-14% is OK for men, and 14-18% for women. If you are overweight and not muscular your body fat will be more. Sagging skin and flab shows your fat %age is more.

2. Aerobic Fitness— It is indicated by the ability to do moderately strenuous activity over a period of time without panting. It reflects how well your heart and lungs work together to supply oxygen to your body during exertion. If you can climb a 6-storey building in a fast pace without panting, or, better, raise your heart beat by 25% (if your beat is 70 raise it to 87-90 by running or brisk walking or cycling and if you can continue doing the exercise at this pace for 5-7 minutes without panting you are fit in this respect.

3. Flexibility— You should have the ability to move any joint through its full range of motion. If you do not do flexibility exercises your joints would be stiff and this is obviously a non-fit condition.

4. Muscle mass— We require a certain per centage of muscle to stay healthy and this varies from individual to individual. With age we lose muscle mass each year and hence it's important to do muscle building exercise to keep muscle mass. Sagging skin and flab is an indication of less muscles.

5. Muscular Endurance— This indicates the ability to hold a particular position for a sustained period of time or repeat a movement many times.

If you can hold a two-kilogram weight above your head for five minutes or lift the same 20 consecutive times you get a pass mark.

6. Static balance— This is your ability to maintain control of your body's centre of gravity over your base of support. This ability helps one from toppling over. You may stand on one leg and hold the other leg 1 foot above and note the time you can do so without losing balance. Anything above 60 seconds is a good measure.

Exercise and be fit

"But let me say that if there is a magic to enhance the quality of your life in general: it is exercise," says Dr. Amy Wechsler, the author of Mind-Beauty Connection. "Exercise fights the onset of age-related diseases, lifts your spirits and sense of well-being, increases your lung capacity so you can take in more oxygen, boosts circulation to deliver nutrients to cells and skin, lowers inflammation, and, for many, it is said to be the ultimate stress reducer. That healthy glow you get after a great workout (rosy cheeks indicative of the increased circulation that is nourishing all those facial cells and tissues) isn't just for show."

There are endless studies on exercise and its mind-body-beauty connection. Exercise makes your brain release certain chemicals with anti-depressant effects. Regular exercise helps to extend your life. Even the middle aged people who start exercising become healthier. In a well-known Harvard alumni study, it was found that 26,000 people who had spent 2000 calories per week by exercising extended their lives by 2 years. Simply put, it was found that every hour of exercise would add three hours of extra life.

All of us know that exercise is good for our body and mind, but even half of us do not want to resort to it regularly. It not only energizes but lifts our spirits too. It helps every single cell of your body by producing chemicals like endorphins that make you peaceful and jovial. It is an anti-dote for insomnia, depression, and is a self -booster. Exercise helps to manage stress better and it simply promotes psychological well-being. People who exercise look toned, healthier and younger as they burn off calories. As weight reduction is inevitable, it wards off hyper tension, protects you from heart disease, obesity, back pain and diabetes. It also helps one maintain healthy bones, muscles and joints. The more sugar you burn the more active you become. It helps to boost your sex life. With the enhanced energy level and better self-esteem sex becomes more enjoyable.

On the whole, it helps your personality and entire life. It is after conducting an extensive study on a considerable number of adults on the effect of aerobic exercise on insomnia that the scientists at the Northwestern University concluded that people could improve their quality of sleep, vitality, and mood with regular exercise.

You must have read somewhere some time that you must do 20-30 minutes of aerobic activity like brisk walking, running, cycling, 3-5 times a week. It is essential too that you engage in some muscle-strengthening activity like stretching at least twice a week. For those who have been inactive for a while, they can start with walking or swimming at a comfortable pace for short periods and slowly and begin more strenuous activities later. Exercise will make you feel hungry and you may eat more food but you will not eat enough to match the calories you burn. There are 700 odd exercises and workouts to choose from.

Our body is a complex machine and every part of it—every muscle, joint and limb needs lubrication and movement. The more we move the better. As we advance in age we move less and our body becomes stiffer and the joints taut. If inactivity continues there comes a point of very little movement and death is at the doorsteps. Movement determines the quality of life. And exercise insures us. Move more and live more healthily. Inactivity and moving less erodes our mental faculties. As the body becomes stiffer the mind begins to rust. The more used and agile your body and limbs the fitter your mind.

Remember the ancient Roman saying, in a sound body rests a sound mind.

When our organs, limbs and joints are not exercised they start giving trouble. Slowly but steadily diseases start coming in. Hospital, doctor, and medicine cripple your life. Regular physical exercise will keep away the doctor.

Those who do not find time for exercise must eventually make time for illness. Those who prefer to be in their comfort zones of idling will end up soon in the cold world 6 feet below.

All of us know what is needed to live healthier and more fulfilling lives. The sad thing is that we do not do what we know. We are waiting for the right or opportune time. And in the process weeks slip into months and months into years. Before long the sun will start casting long shadows signaling the downing of the curtain and there will be a lurking regret that we did not live life the best way we could. There is no need to find a well-equipped gym to begin exercising. You could start walking on your terrace in a round, as I do every day, watching the painted cotton puffs floating in the sky, savouring the fragrance in the breeze, feasting on the western picture post card like painting of nature against the city skyline, watching the crimson ball slowly lowering below the horizon. The fresh air, the chirpings of nestling birds and the slow darkening process will be, in themselves, invigorating.

The latest fad is gyro tonics— a form of physical alignment and deep muscle control. It basically consists of about 50 exercises which involve bending, stretching, twisting, and turning the muscle and skeletal system. It requires the latest machinery and is offered at selected health centres. But if you don't have such a centre nearby you, there is nothing to worry as the good-old exercises are more than enough. There is no evidence to suggest that the high-tech-one mentioned here is any better than the accepted aerobic, muscle building and flexible exercises mentioned before.

Remember, life begins at the end of your comfort zone. You need to start putting effort to make your body an efficient and well-oiled machine. To enjoy the glow of good health and a good personality, you must exercise.

Chapter-11

Take the first step; the next step follows

"Cowards never start, the weak never finish, winners never quit."

—Ainsley Rodriguez

A journey of a thousand miles begins with a single step. But without making that first step nothing will be accomplished. Once the first step is taken the next one and the next and all the others may simply fall in line. You already have enough to begin with that first step. If you are looking for alibis of 'if only' you will never really start anything or reach anywhere. If you keep on thinking about the problems ahead, you may tend to postpone things. Prolonged delay paralyses any initiative you might have had. There is no auspicious day, there is no special circumstance; every day is right and every moment is auspicious.

All the conditions will not be just right and perfect conditions will never arrive. What you can do now in the present is set-up all that really matters. The distant and the vague appeals to the human mind as no specific action needs to be taken. It is difficult to take the first steps but remember, you unleash a lot of power in doing so.

"The lure of the distant and the difficult is deceptive; the great opportunity is here," says, John Burroughs, the American writer.

From what I know of the lives of great personalities, I can tell you that everything great they have achieved had begun with something very insignificant. And many people have not achieved anything simply because they failed to take that first step.

The impossible is many a time the untried. If you are in grave doubt or worry about when or how to start the journey, just take the first step and get past the starting point. Subsequent steps would follow and you may reach a point of no return! You already have enough to take the first step and then the next. Do not worry what will happen tomorrow. Take the first step and then the next and go on.

Before we begin a new venture the whole project looks so very overbearing that we are thwarted. When you look at the long road ahead, the destination looks far away and the task daunting. And you do not feel like starting the operation at all. Suppose you are overweight and you want to reduce 30kgs. You think about the rigorous exercises over a long period of time, the food control measures that have to be implemented and you become dispirited. It is easier to be the way you are: eat whatever you want, do not exercise and it is easy to remain in your comfort zone. But all that you need to do is to just take one step now. Begin your journey. Start with a simple exercise. Do not look too far ahead or too far back either. **Enjoy your present exercise.**

If you have begun, you have overcome the inertia and that is a great achievement. Once you start there is a momentum to push you for a little while and a few steps would definitely follow. You have to get charged up by motivating yourself with the goal thereafter. Once it is an intense desire more steps would follow. March on never losing sight of the finish line and never looking back. When I was a faculty of the TKM college of engineering in 1976, State Bank of Travancore had an offer: deposit Rs1000/- and get 100,000 after 40 years. I thought about it for a long time. But looking so far ahead into the future everything looked hazy and impractical. I held on with the idea for quite some time but never took the first step. And the result: I saved nothing. Now after about 40 years, I regret having not taken that first step. I could have easily deposited Rs50,000/- over a period of a few years and I would have been a millionaire now!

We hear people talking about big plans over and over in life. There are so many who want to write books and become famous, others who want to start a big business, and still others who plan to build a mansion. They are all waiting for the conditions to become right, for the auspicious moment. Very few realize that every moment is auspicious and every day is the right day. The conditions are not going to be different from what it is now the next year or after ten years. If you do not put that first step, you will never achieve what you want. As in the case of my savings plan I would have been closer to my goal had I acted on time and started depositing my savings in the bank. If you wait under whatever pretext, the goal would recede further and further without any change in your conditions.

Winning is the most important part of any endeavour. ***Non-starter is worse than a quitter.*** *90% of success lies in starting, in taking the first step. You may fail after starting but you have a chance to win. If you do not start you are doomed as you have no chance to win. The first step is the hardest of all. Many of us fail because we do not take that first step. We do not overcome the inertia. One step is all that matters. If you don't grow, you whither; no one can stand still. In other words you will never do great things if you do not* *do small things. The courage to begin is the same as the courage required to win. Little by little is a universal rule. Doing small things like taking that first step makes all the difference in life.*

We know our health and hence personality very much depends on our mental condition. When we are in the company of good people or are in cheerful surroundings, our bodies function much better. Unpleasant scenery and the presence of those whom we dislike can make us sick and tired. A steady, good state of mind can usher in health and sickness.

Mental states influence our nervous system and vital organs. One can acquire radiant health with a bit of exercise and food control coupled with a positive state of mind.

It is now proven mental disturbances like anxiety and tension can induce diabetes, asthma, bronchitis and even blood pressure. Acute depressions and intense grieving can induce cancers! One's feelings, emotions, and mental states reflected in one's brain waves, influence our health. Simply put, mind has a lot to do with one's physical state. By controlling one's mind one can be healthy.

Depressing and negative thoughts force our glands secrete poison into the blood. It affects or retards the normal body functions like circulation, digestion and assimilation. A pleasant state of mind induces positive secretions which facilitate all these functions.

Chapter-12

How to attain super health?

"It is health that is real wealth and not pieces of gold and silver."

—Mahatma Gandhi

"To keep the body in good health is a duty... otherwise we shall not be able to keep our mind strong and clear."

—Buddha

There is no point in living without being healthy.

Does your health depend on the treatment you receive to cure your diseases?

Does it depend on the number of times you visit doctors or hospitals?

Doctors, hospitals and medication can only help you get rid of symptoms of diseases. And, absence of disease is not health.

There are 3 stages in this: Diseases, absence of diseases and super health. Generally people are worried about the first stage and are interested in the second one. Super health is perfect mental and physical well-being. Very few are even aware of the third stage and still less know that it is purely based on a personal initiative.

You can be mentally and physically fit only if you want to, only if you think and intensely desire it. Medical examinations and tests will reveal certain parametres like blood pressure, sugar and cholesterol levels in the blood, the onslaught of cancer, AIDS, or any other disease and the way your heart, lungs, kidney, liver or any other vital organ functions. The doctors will advise you as to how to get rid of adverse symptoms and prescribe medication to get rid of them. But they don't tell you how to be super-healthy.

No doctor can make you super healthy. No medication can ensure your mental and physical well-being nor can it induce youthfulness and energy. No one else can lead you into great health but you.

Your thoughts will decide whether you will be healthy or sick, young or old.

Maybe the following checklist would help:

- Do you have an intense desire to live long and healthy?

- Do you have a life goal or goals which will drive you forward and make you fruitfully engaged always?
- Do you control your diet? Eat generally less, eat more vegetables, fruits, whole grains and nuts; take less salt and sugar, drink more water; avoid fatty and fried foods.
- Are you physically fit?
- Do you exercise your brain and memory on a regular basis? (see the chapter on strengthening your memory).
- Do you feel like involving yourself romantically with those of the opposite sex of any age?
- Do you enjoy your life and feel grateful to the forces that gave birth to you?
- Do you take care of your personal appearance?
- Do you find leisure time to go for picnics and keep friendship with like-minded people?

Have you noticed a few of your co-workers and friends who never seem to get sick? They seem to enjoy good health while everyone around them is sneezing and coughing. What calms their minds and relieves stress? What has strengthened their hearts and lungs? What makes them healthy and fit?

What is the problem with you? You may be overweight, clumsy and tired all the time. You may be feeling less energetic, lethargic and sick. Is the charm of living ebbing away? Decide now to be super healthy. **Your thoughts and beliefs determine the condition of your own body.**

You have to realize that health is the foundation upon which all good things of your life are built. You need to decide that excellent health is your number-one priority always.

An excellent diet and consistent exercise are still the most important habits you need to cultivate, but if you want them to stick, then you need to make some internal shifts first.

Start picturing yourself as super healthy. May be you can tell yourself each day twice or thrice that you are in perfect health both in body and mind. Just after waking up and just before going to bed at night, close your eyes, take a few deep, slow breaths and count from ten to one. Then visualize in your mind's eye yourself enjoying perfect health, feel super strong and energized. Open your eyes feeling happy with the surge of heath and energy. Read inspirational material that can motivate you on the benefits of becoming super healthy.

Try to make friends with super healthy people or with those who really want to. Avoid negative ones, who have the attitude, 'Oh, it does not matter; life is so short and hence let us eat, drink and enjoy.'

Do not compromise on sleep. Get lots of it and have some leisure time. There is no dispute on the positive effects of smiling and laughing more. It will relieve you from stress and make you happier.

Some other things you might take care are mentioned below:

- Keep your mind quiet for about 10-20 minutes each day.
- Stretch and do flexibility exercises on a regular basis.
- Do something you love each day for some time.
- Have a positive frame of mind and take things lightly.
- Get some achievements each day— however small they may be.
- Exercise for at least half an hour or more—jog, brisk walk, cycle and swim— every day.
- Work more—do more than you are paid for.

Of course quit smoking and avoid too much alcohol. Gargling regularly with an antiseptic mouthwash helps to improve dental health and may keep off flu and cold. There is no need for anyone to worry; 90% of all your worry does not happen. The remaining 10% or so will happen whether you worry or not.

Clean up your diet, and start exercising. A holistic approach to exercise will calm your mind and relieve stress; lung-cardio strengthening exercises will help boost your immune system. Whenever circulation is increased, you get far more white blood cells; they will gobble up the foreign harmful germs in the blood. A positive frame of mind will induce your glands to pump beneficial secretions into your blood stream.

Eating better and exercising more with an intense desire to be super-healthy is the magic wand to become perfectly healthy both in body and mind.

❖❖

Chapter-13

Sports and you

Playing a sport is undoubtedly a fun activity and is a source of great entertainment. But did you know that regular sporting activities not only take care of your physical fitness but also enhance your personality and help you in maintaining your mental well-being?

Playing sports helps much more than just in the physical aspects. It builds character, teaches strategic and analytical thinking, leadership skills, goal setting and risk taking and many others. Sports require discipline, assertiveness and the ability to work as a team and a willingness to compete without fear of failure.

These positive characteristic traits help you at your workplace, as well as in your interpersonal relationships.

The ancient Greeks, who developed philosophy and arts, also took sport seriously. They encouraged people to develop strong, fit and graceful bodies. Men and boys would compete in running, jumping, discus and javelin throwing competitions.

Leading psychologists feel playing any kind of sport brings out the leader in you. You learn to handle pressure and perform in any circumstance. Sports makes you bring out your inner most reserves of energy and other resources to perform the extra-ordinarily.

How do sports help us?

- Participating in sports develops strength, speed, skill, stamina and flexibility.
- When we are under stress/anxiety, work pressures, playing sports helps release them.
- Sports are always fun.
- It instills a sense of well-being.
- Help us sleep better.
- Develops motor skills and mind/body connection.
- Helps overcome depression.
- Reduces risk of many diseases.

- Helps build character.
- Improves leadership skills.
- Encourages risk taking.

Games improve teamwork. Any game requires co-coordinating with a number of people as a team. It helps you perform better at your workplace; especially if you are required to work with a group of people.

Improves self-esteem and builds confidence. Perhaps, the most important quality sports can inculcate in you is self-esteem and confidence. You learn to take success and failure in the right spirit. One trains himself to be strong and to focus fully on the game. This will in turn help you focus in other aspects.

Provides relief from stress. When you are bogged down with work, playing some sort of sport helps you stay stress-free and happy. Neurotransmitters present in your brain cells are stimulated as you exercise and it is believed that these transmitters help your moods and emotions.

Improves concentration and time management skills. Those who are into sports, learn to manage time efficiently. They start valuing the importance of time more in their lives. Sports help you prepare, schedule, and prioritize your deadlines well and this builds your time management skills.

Children should play sports

Today most of our children are stuck with a TV or computer. You might encourage your child to play sports because being physically active is good for their mind and body.

Children who play sports might also learn character and behaviour traits that help develop their personalities. Not even one in three children is active in sports these days. Fitness experts feel that getting your kids involved in playing sports will help them get more active and, perhaps, develop a healthier personality.

According to the American Academy of Child and Adolescent Psychiatry, playing a sport can help improve a child's self-esteem. It requires physical, mental and emotional endurance to compete. Children learn motivation, determination, and they get the long-term benefits of training and working towards a goal. The feeling of accomplishment as they build their athletic skills improves self-esteem, a very important personality trait.

Children acquire better social skills. Playing a team sport helps kids bond with each other. A web page on the University of Florida website cites research by the Institute for the Study of Youth Sports found that children who play sports have better social skills. Playing a sport requires cooperation with others. They learn to play fair while having fun with others and work towards a common goal. Children might also develop a healthy sense of competition. All these give them better skills to interact with others at school and at home.

They develop Leadership skills. Getting to practise on time and with all the required equipment is always a challenge. Although kids have to be coaxed out of bed or away from the TV, he will soon learn to manage to be on time to practise and play the game. Playing a sport also teaches children to take on other leadership roles such as handling conflict, developing game strategies and encouraging team members.

They learn to cope up with emotions. There will be emotional highs and lows in any game. Learning to cope up with them in a healthy manner is a valuable personality trait for children as well as adults. Playing a sport gives the players experiences of joy and excitement after a win and grief and frustration after a loss. Sports teach children to bounce back and try again after a failure. They learn that sometimes, even though they might play their best, their team will lose. Playing a sport gives all an environment where coaches and team members can provide encouragement and help to build resilience.

Chapter-14

Develop self-confidence

What makes people hesitant from pursuing their dreams is the lack of self-confidence and fear of failure. This is debilitating and has to be overcome. But then how do you do that?The simple way is to work on developing self-confidence.

If you are low in self-confidence, is it possible to do things that will change that? I was very shy as a child with tons of inferiority complex and I was not confident in anything. Tried some of these simple tips mentioned here for years and that's what helped me overcome my fears and pursue my dreams. Some of those fears are still lurking inside, but I have learnt how to beat them and do what I want.

If you feel shy, diffident, not smart, attractive or competent, don't lose hope. Psychologists and other experts do believe that you can do things to improve all of them. Self-confidence is not genetic, and you can rely on yourself to build it and other personality attributes over a period of time.

Some people make a strong distinction between self-esteem and self-confidence. Here we use them interchangeably.

You can become someone worthy of respect, someone who can pursue what he wants despite your shortcomings. You can do this by taking control of your life and what you do or how you spend your time.

There is no magic to shred off your diffidence. But there are certain practical steps which might be of help to develop it. I outline below 22 mantras that will help you build self-confidence.

1. "Do it now" is an old principle. Do not postpone things; finish today's work today itself. If there are a lot of things to do, make a priority schedule and do the most urgent ones today and the rest at start of the next day.

2. Save some money from whatever you earn and let it grow in the bank. Having something in there gives a feeling of confidence. On the other hand, if you have to borrow from someone, it will erode your confidence.

3. Help a stranger without expecting anything in return. It can be helping a blind cross the road, giving a little money to a poor person you do not know, consoling an aggrieved friend, removing a thistle or a boulder from the road (so that someone else will not be hurt) or helping a stranger who is in real trouble.

4. Work on small things. Trying to take on a huge project or task can be overwhelming, daunting and intimidating for anyone, even the best of us. Instead, learn to break off large tasks into small chunks and complete each one. Small, little achievements make you feel good, and they add up to big achievements. Learn to work like this all the time, and soon you'll be self-confident.

5. Do not entertain guilt. We have all done a number of wrong things in the past when we were young or immature. There could be many reasons; many of them were well beyond our control, there could have been adverse home and environmental influences too. There is no point in crying over what has already happened. Forget the past. Learn lessons from them and move on. But do not repeat the same mistakes again. There is no need to feel guilty about anything. The only sin in the world is harming or paining another person. And if you have committed those sins you cannot do anything about it now. Ask forgiveness and move on with a determination not to commit such follies again.

6. Always be smartly dressed and groomed. Prefer designer wear. Go in for dresses which suites your complexion and appearance. You need not be crazy after fashion or what others seem to like. Choose your attire-something you enjoy and feel good about. Take care of personal hygiene: shower, shave, comb your hair, apply makeup and perfume (if you feel good) and let everything you put on be well-thought about, appropriate for the context, nice and neatly pressed. Let your footwear be nicely polished and presentable.

If you dress nicely, you'll feel good about yourself. You'll feel successful, good and ready to tackle the world. It doesn't necessarily mean you wear very expensive clothes, but wear clothes that are good, appropriate to the context, and professional.

7. Try to do more than you are paid for. Do not try to do the bare minimum to keep the job. "Go the extra mile." Your extra work will never go waste. The Universe will reward you a hundred fold. And it will boost your self-esteem. When you work more than what you are expected of, you will start feeling you are a good person.

8. Get active. Doing something is almost always better than doing nothing. Utilize your free time constructively and ensure you do not remain at the bottom for long. When you simply sit idling away your time or loiter with friends doing nothing, you will gather a feeling that you are almost useless. You need to be also purposefully engaged-doing things to further your aims.

9. Keep your strengths always highlighted in your mind and downplay weakness. Everyone has strengths and flaws. Make an inventory of your assets. Just start writing down right now the good qualities you possess.

It could be:

- Your IQ;
- Hardworking nature;
- Organized ways;
- Ability to make friends;
- Reading/learning habit;
- Honesty;
- Ambition;
- Smartness;
- Care in personal appearance;
- Integrity;
- Ability to connect with others;
- Saving mentality;
- Drive;
- Courage;
- Loving dear ones;
- Pleasing nature;
- Patience;
- Love of details;
- Ability to control emotions.

Well, mention anything and everything you consider good in you. Your list can go on ....let the list be exhaustive. Keep the file open for a few days and ask those whom you know well to help you. Once a comprehensive list is prepared, type them out neatly and go through the list every now and then: at least once just before sleeping and once just after waking up.

10. Become fit and healthy. Your weight should be ideal or as per your Body Mass Index. Eat less, exercise well, and keep yourself fit. A clumsy person cannot feel confident easily. The healthier, fitter and more agile you are, the better your confidence levels.

11. Maintain peak state body physiology. Keep a confident posture. Sit, stand, and walk erect with drawn shoulders and head held high. Always adopt an open posture—palms held open, hands held slightly away from your body and legs held apart. Do not be in closed positions. Learn more on this from the chapter on body language. Let your movements be brisk. Wrong body postures and lethargic moves will make your mind lethargic too.

12. Make sure of a small success each day. It can be advancing towards your goal by whatever small fraction, taking a positive step towards self-confidence or updating yourself in your chosen field. Even a decision to use your free time purposefully is a 'win'. So is stopping rumour-mongering or talking bad about anybody. Instead, talk something good about a guy to your friends. Sit a little time more in the office to work. Help your family a little more.

13. Expect setbacks/failures but keep a smile. Remember, without fighting adversities or failures no one has gone up. There will be temporary failures, unpleasant experiences. These are all part of life. Still keep a smile all the time. Smiling works to make you feel instantly better. When you smile —it helps you and others as well. It has a chain reaction of spreading happiness and overcoming anxiety. The moment your facial muscles develop into a smile the tension you feel about anything simply melts down. Not convinced? Try it now.

14. Try to keep your dear ones always happy. Spend quality time with your family and kids. Sacrifice something or the other so that they are happier. Get what they love most without grudge. If you can stop finding fault with your spouse that will be a great step to a fulfilling life. Do anything possible to see that your family is happy. If they are unhappy or feel you don't care, you can never feel confident.

15. Think positive, avoid negative thoughts. Prefer positive minded friends and avoid negative or pessimistic ones. Friends can make or break you. You should learn to replace negative thoughts with positive ones. You have to learn to be aware of your self-talk, the thoughts you have about yourself and what you're doing. Kill any negative thought that surfaces with a mental effort (ask it to get away) and replace it with a positive one.

16. Keep your focus on your goals. Let them guide you like the North Star. Set a small goal and achieve it. People often make the mistake of dreaming big when they fail and they get discouraged easily. Set a goal you know you can achieve and get it. Naturally when you get it, you will feel good. Now set another one, slightly larger and achieve that. The more goals you achieve, the better your confidence levels become.

It can be anything like waking up 10 minutes earlier or drinking a glass of water when you wake up. Something small that you know you can do.

Do it for a month. When you've accomplished it, you'll feel much more confident to achieve more.

17. Speak slowly. It has a big difference in how others perceive you. A person in authority speaks slowly. It shows confidence. A person who feels that he isn't worth listening to, will speak quickly. Even if you don't feel the confidence of someone who speaks slowly, try to speak slower few times a day at least.

18. Fix the principles upon which your life is built. You have to know them. Otherwise your life will be directionless. You may like to be truthful, honest, caring and helping all the time. Or you may desire to reach the highest office in your corporation. Know your life principles and try to live them. You can decide to think, say and do good always as a life-principle. When you engage in rumour mongering or are intentionally telling lies, you are eroding your own self-worth feelings.

19. Be grateful for everything to your parents, home, teachers, school, relatives, neighbours, friends, colleagues, boss, company, universe. This world has given life to you in this 21st century and you enjoy the fruit of man's civilization and advancements in science and technology. Your parents have brought you up with love, so have your relatives. The school and university have helped you learn. You have a lot to be thankful for. Developing a grateful attitude is a big boost for esteem levels.

So many think they got a raw deal in life. Their home was poor, parents never cared. Inheritance was poor too. But what are you going to gain by projecting these? None loves to hear your deficiencies. The world goes with the winner; it doesn't care about your misfortunes or childhood inadequacies. Irrespective of all that, win you must. And without confidence how can you do it? There is so much in you—for that matter in anybody— to be thankful for. Feel gratitude to have got birth, for this life, for everything.

20. Acquire general and specialized knowledge. When you get more and more knowledge, it empowers you and is one of the best strategies for building self-confidence. Read newspapers, get knowledge from the net, blogs, TV programmes and by interacting with others. You need to develop a world-view. You cannot be confined to one set of beliefs or faith. Reach out to others, know them, know the origin and destination of this earth, this life. The way religions and various philosophies and political thoughts evolved.

21. Get rid of unpleasant and past experiences. There must have been a lot of past unpleasant experiences in your life just like in anybody else's. We have to learn to throw them away from our minds. Experiences stay; put or opt to leave depending on how we entertain them. If we accentuate them they get impressed and they refuse to leave; if we fade them into insignificance they simply disappear.

If you recall an unpleasant past experience in colour, make it black and white and fade it further into a defused state. See the entire thing far away from your mind. Lower the pitch of the sounds you hear and let them echo from afar. Let the feeling part be made insignificant. Make the whole experience small and then smaller. If it was the size of a football earlier bring it down to the size of a cricket ball and still smaller may be to the size of a pin head. Then you throw it out of your mind. Now it has very little impact on you. The faint defused echoes of something will altogether disappear. Fill the space thus created with a positive experience. Let your mind be filled with powerful experiences enabling you to become more confident.

22. Get to know yourself: Keep in mind Sun Tzu's famous observation, *'Know yourself and you will win all battles.'* A wise general learns his enemy very well. You can't defeat the enemy without knowing him. And when you're trying to overcome a negative self-image and replace it with self-confidence, your enemy is yourself. Get to know yourself well.

Start listening to your thoughts. What thoughts you have about yourself, and analyze why you have such negative thoughts. Think about the good things about yourself, the things you can do well, the things you like. Find out your negative points just enough to correct them and not to brood over or feel bad about. Once you sufficiently know yourself, move on ahead with all the tools mentioned here.

Pretend you are courageous –sometimes this helps. And if you act to be confident (while you are not) on a regular basis you will become so.

During a presidential election campaign, **Nelson Mandela's** propeller plane developed a snag a few minutes before landing. But he continued to be calm reading a newspaper. The plane had an emergency landing and Mandela came out safe. Later he revealed to a reporter: **'Man, I was terrified up there. Of course I was afraid. But as a leader you cannot let people know it. You must put up a front.'** Even by acting he could inspire others. If you are not confident at a particular juncture, pretend you are.

Self-esteem and social relationship

Psychological research has consistently shown the relationship between one's self esteem and his social relationship. A high confidence level helps one to live spontaneously and be successful socially. A low confidence level makes one more guarded and critical of others.

Yes, that's the key. Being confident about who you are and what you are doing is the most important tip for personality development. Never doubt your capabilities and if there is something you need to work upon then put in all the effort so you can come over your fears and gain confidence. Read success stories or surround yourself with motivational thoughts or "encouragements" which can boost up your self-esteem and help you in attaining a confident personality.

Confidence is what makes one successful in life. Although its levels have a bearing on one's heredity, home, early school and neighbourhood influences, one can develop it at any stage in life if one wants to. Apart from the points discussed above, keeping your family happy is of critical importance. The more positive vibes you send out, the more will be your self-worth feelings. Being honest and keeping the interest of your company is helpful too. Try to be friendly to all and avoid friction with colleagues, people under you and superiors.

"Somehow I can't believe that there are any heights that can't be scaled by a man who knows the secrets of making dreams come true. This special secret, it seems to me, can be summarized in four C's. They are curiosity, confidence, courage, and constancy, and the greatest of all is confidence. When you believe in a thing, believe in it all the way, implicitly and unquestionably."

—Walt Disney

Chapter-15

Body language and personality

"People need realness, reality. People can sense when someone is being pretentious or fake. It's because you feel it; you see it in someone's body language."

—Afrojack

Some basic signs and their meanings

- **The shoulder shrug—** It is a universal gesture to indicate indifference.
- **The Ring or 'OK' Gesture—** When you display a circle formed with your forefinger and thumb shows, OK, excellent or perfect.
- **The Thumb-Up Gesture—** It is commonly used by hitch-hikers for a lift. It is also used to indicate encouragement and appreciation.

- **Covering mouth/ears, touching nose/ neck, putting finger in ears, across lips—** All normally mean what you say is a lie.
- **Head nod—** It can mean 'yes' and 'no' depending on the context.
- **Folded hands—** (at the back or front) Shows negativity, skepticism, blocking the message he receives.
- **Hands on your hip—** This is to make yourself seem bigger, more threatening, convincing or influential.
- **Hands behind your back or in front—** One holding the other by the forearm denotes insecurity, mistrust, fear.
- **Hands placed on the other person's shoulder—** You try to draw him to your side.
- **Playing with hair, objects such as wine glass stem—** A finger, a cocktail glass or any other such thing signifies romantic feelings.

- **Feet and hands crossed—** While sitting down means you have retreated from the discussion and have no interest in what is discussed or in the other person.
- If your legs are oriented in a different direction away from the other when you talk with someone means that you want to end the discussion and move in the direction shown by your feet.
- **Glass or pen placed in mouth while listening—** It denotes a state of uncertainty.
- **Hand to the forehead or head—** It signifies shame, embarrassment or hiding from the world.
- **Head held in the palm—** It denotes boredom.
- **Fist to face—** It means appreciation for the listener.
- **Lifting eyebrows—** To express disbelief.
- **Clasp your arms—** To isolate or protect yourself.
- **Slap forehead—** It means forgetting.
- **Tightly clenched hand—** It shows frustration and hostility.

Body language (BL) which is best defined as a non-verbal form of communication—expressed through body, face, gestures, eye movements, posture, and body movements—speak a lot about one's personality. In essence, if you want to achieve an effective personality, you will also need to improve your body language.

Body language does not have a grammar and must be interpreted broadly, instead of having an absolute meaning corresponding with a certain movement, there are agreed-upon interpretations of a particular behaviour. These may vary from country to country, or culture to culture but there are aspects in it considered to have the same meaning or interpretation universally.

Our postures and gestures have something to say about us, e.g., leaning forward while making a point signals over-assertiveness or aggression; lying back on your seat while an important discussion is a cold signal boredom or apathy; keeping your hands on your waist while talking to someone could signal confrontation, and so on.

There are many ways you can improve body language, but like most things, it needs practise and consistency so that it will become part of you, and not just something you can do for a certain period of time. If you want to develop your personality in a positive way, you need to be aware of your own body language first and make sure it adheres to what is generally perceived as **positive body language.**

Body language and emotions

Combinations of postures, gestures, general bearing, facial expressions, eye, lip and cheek movements— help form different moods of an individual—

happy, confident, sad, depressed, angry and so on. Judging emotions based on facial expressions is fairly accurate; emotions can also be detected through body postures. A person feeling angry would portray dominance over the other, clench fists, bare teeth, and his/her posture displays approach tendencies. If, on the other hand, one is fearful or diffident he/she would feel weak, submissive and his/her posture would display avoidance tendencies. If a person leans forward with his/her head nodding shows his interest in the conversation and if he leans back tending to look elsewhere he does not have interest in it. A person who has his/her legs and arms crossed with the foot kicking slightly implies that he/she is feeling impatient and emotionally detached from the discussion.

Each emotion that we feel inwardly is always expressed by a set of body movements and expressions. Facial expressions and body postures always indicate inner emotions. When one feels fearful, anxious, depressed or sad his body language will indicate the mental state: droops body, looks down, lips tremble, and eyes droop without focusing anywhere with flat or monotone speech, close arms and legs and adopt slower movements. When one is happy and confident, he/she stands or sits erect, looks straight or slightly upward, facial and body muscles get more relaxed, and assumes an open body position.

Confidence indicators

Erect, open posture— head held high, drawn shoulders, looking straight, arms open and held slightly away from body—with brisk movements indicate a confident person. But one who drops his shoulders, looking down, in a closed position (arms folded at the back or front, and legs held closer with clumsy or slow movements indicate the individual lacks self-confidence.

How to alter inner emotions?

Inner emotional state is mirrored by your body. By changing your body language your inner mental state can be altered too. If say, you are in a very sad or fearful state of mind, your body almost immediately assumes postures, gestures and muscle movements to suite this mental state. If you change your body language you will see how it affects your feelings.

Instead of dropping your body, straighten it, stand or sit erect, hold your head high and look straight, relax your facial muscles, breathe deep and slow and try a smile and move brisker. Instantly your fear and sadness will fade and a more confident feeling would be ushered in. The reverse is true too. Change your confident body posture: droop it, draw your limbs closer to body, sit hunch backed looking down, let your eyes not focus anywhere, let breath become shallow and fast and make your movements slow and listless. You will immediately feel sad or fearful.

If you want to achieve an effective personality, you will need to be always in a confident state of mind by improving your body language. There are many ways to do it. You need to be aware of your own body language and make sure you adopt confident postures, facial expressions, gestures, brisk movements, deep-slow breathing, smart dressing and grooming-what is generally perceived as **positive body language.**

We have already discussed **Barrack Obama** and how he conducts himself. You may think he being a very confident, positive and assertive person, his body language conforms to his inner nature. But the reverse is true too. **If you adopt confident postures, gestures, brisk movements, smart dressing and grooming all the time, you will become confident, smart and positive.** But changing you habitual postures, ways of movements and general bearing will take effort and time. But then nothing is achieved without sweat, determination and hard work. Adopt better body postures, better ways of physical appearance, looking, talking and moving so that you are always in a confident state. Even faking powerful body language reduces stress and makes you more confident.

If you are always frowning, this would indicate that you have a negative aura, and this will push others away. Whereas if you are constantly seen smiling, you are going to attract other sunny and happy people to yourself. You need to sit properly, avoid slouching, and if you can, keep an open posture at all times, leaning towards the speaker whenever necessary, to show that you are interested.

Try to avoid these

- **Fidgeting.** This would only indicate your nervousness and will make others doubt your ability.
- **Standing too close.** When you are too close to someone, physically, it will make the other person uncomfortable and will also trigger them to think you are invading their personal space.
- **Staring.** Staring is considered to be rude. While you maintain eye contact towards the other person, do not overdo it and stare.
- **A fake smile—creating wrinkle only at the corner of the mouth without creating wrinkles at the corner of the eyes is** very negative.
- **Absence of personal hygiene and shabby dressing and grooming.**

- **Crossing your arms.** This would indicate resistance on your part, so if someone is talking to you and you are crossing your arms, you will make the other person think that you really are not agreeing to what he says.
- **Avoiding eye-contact.** People with low self-esteem try to keep away from making eye-contact. They tend to look down or away from the person. They'll only look you in the eye for a second then dart away. Learn to look straight into the eyes of the person you have a conversation with.
- **Bad postures.** This is the most obvious of the body language sign of a desperate or sad guy. Hunched shoulders and body, looking down, engaged in negative self-talk are indications. They move slow and clumsy, shake hands with no energy or enthusiasm with no interest in their personal attire or appearance.
- **Being small, taking less space.** Look at how a person stands, how apart are his legs. A confident person will stand with legs at about shoulder width apart. If you imagine a superhero like Superman, he shows extreme confidence by having an extra wide stance beyond his shoulders. A non-confident person will take up as little space as possible and stand with their feet close together. Putting shoulders together is another body language tactic to be smaller and take up less space.

Legs and emotions

The lower legs display often a person's feelings. Your feet are the parts of your body that balance you, that take you in the direction you want to go. The angle at which your feet are facing can indicate what kind of feelings you have. Imagine a conversation between a man and a woman in a dinner party. Her feet are angled away from him and towards the front door. It is more than likely that she does not want to be talking to him, and would much rather leave! This is an instinctual response; people will often point their feet towards things that they want or like and away from things they don't.

Defensive body language

Most normal people like to be closer to people they like and further away from people they don't like. Human body language can very clearly show whom we want to be near and whom we don't, but it may be more complicated than simply leaning towards or away from someone. People might simply close themselves indicating they don't want to share anything. Folding your arms across your chest, assuming a closed body posture, crossing your legs while sitting are all to keep away others. You are creating a barrier for the other person.

Breathing and you

The most significant body language signal that tells us how a person really feels is reflected in their breathing patterns. Studies show that each emotional state has a specific breathing pattern associated with it. A recent study has brought the use of breathing as a way to control emotions. Does breathing generate and regulate emotions and their intensity? Experts think they do.

Check your breath patterns

- When you are in panic, you breathe short, fast and shallow.
- When you are in anger, you take long and forced breaths.
- When you are calm, you have slow and steady breaths.
- When you are happy you have long inhalations and long exhalations.

Extensive studies indicate that breathing really does affect one's emotional state. It means that there is now another tried and tested method for controlling our emotional state. Controlling emotions by regulating breathing undoubtedly requires discipline and diligence. The moment you change your fast shallow breaths to long, deep and slow ones you feel happier and your fearful or anxious state disappears. But if you return to your previous pattern—short, fast and shallow breaths—feeling of panic will return.

Are you lying?

People sometimes lie and their body language will indicate if they are lying.

- When you are lying you may try to block your mouth/words with your hands. Sometimes it can be one finger across the lips.
- A lying individual my rub their eyes while they lie.
- A lying person may cover their ears or drill their finger into an ear.
- Others are seen touching/scratching their nose or neck while speaking.
- A lying person may not look straight into your eyes but look here and there.
- He will not speak straight but falter and grope for words.
- A child may try to withdraw from you instead of facing you squarely.

Make your body language work for you when you meet others

Learn how to use body language to influence others or create the right impact at first sight. Practise some of the following:

1. **Cross nothing:** Keep arms, legs and feet relaxed and uncrossed. If you wear a jacket open it up to give the message I am open and honest with you.

2. **Lean slightly forward:** Interested people always pay attention and lean slightly forward. Never lean backward. It shows withdrawal or no-interest.
3. **Mirror to get positive results.** Pay attention to others' postures, gestures and the way they talk. Is it fast or slow? High-pitched or bass? Then you bring your speech to match it. Adopt their postures as far as possible too.
4. **Have eye-contact:** Direct eye-contact is a compliment to most people to build trust in you.
5. **Handshake:** Not too hard or too soft. But let it be firm displaying warmth and energy. People with low self-esteem have a limp hand shake. A very hard handshake is often painful and negative. No one likes the lifeless fish-like touch. An effective handshake with a warm smile is the best way.
6. **Take care of your appearance each day.** It matters a lot in creating a first impression and the way you feel about yourself.
7. **Keep a pleasant facial expression with a smile.** Face is the most expressive part of the human body. If you are anxious or fearful your facial expression will repel others. You can always overcome a negative facial expression by smiling sincerely. It will make you appear warm, friendly, open and confident.
8. **Have a relaxed posture standing, sitting erect,** shoulders almost drawn, head held straight, leaning towards the person a little make you look confident and interested in others. By leaning back or away from him/her you show a lack of interest. If you hunch your shoulders or keep your head down you display diffidence and lack of courage.
9. **Become approachable:** It is easy to seem unapproachable. Crossing arms on the chest indicates that you are on the defensive. Conversely, a relaxed stance, one where you open your arms and expose your front to the speaker, makes him or her more comfortable and more ready to share their thoughts.
10. **Listen carefully:** The speaker is likely to offer more if the recipient is keen. Show your counterpart that you are interested in what he or she says by leaning to him or her and by nodding your head appropriately. Leaning away shows your disinterest.
11. **Face the speaker:** This allows him to observe your facial expressions. Look at him with interest. You should mirror his/her gestures

with appropriate head shakes to communicate your empathy and appreciation of the message.

12. **Give people your full attention:** Show warmth to people that you are approachable, caring and empathetic. Take people as brothers and sisters. Be curious about them. Warmth is conveyed first from your happiness in meeting him. Let people feel good—not cold or indifferent. Compliment the other person often.
13. **Give a good handshake:** Touch is one of the best ways we can convey warmth to another person. Let your handshake show happiness, warmth and positive energy.
14. **Relax your posture:** You need not strictly erect or it will make you stiff and cold. Let your shoulders, head, muscles assume a natural and comfortable position. Open up your body. Use open body language to communicate warmth to others.
15. **No crossing:** Don't cross your arms across your body, keep them by your side; instead of crossing your legs, leave them open; instead of having a desk or podium between you and the other person, remove barriers.
16. **Have kind eyes:** It's a friendly gaze that some people give to make others feel warm, accepted and understood.
17. **Smile** is an easy way not only to convey warmth to others, but it will make you warm yourself.
18. **Research has shown that a little touch** here and there can do wonders—something like a pat at the back, or arms.
19. **Do not encroach personal space** and create discomfort.
20. **Lower your voice** to convey more authority. The researchers looked at 792 U.S. chief executives at public companies. After controlling for experience, education, and other influential factors, they found that a drop of 22 Hz in voice frequency correlated with an increase of $187,000 in compensation.

One's bearing has a lot to do with what he/she will be in life. A **well-dressed** guy with confident postures creates a first good impression anywhere he goes. Each one has to follow acceptable dressing for professional, social and entertainment contexts. Personal **grooming**—hair, face, manicure, pedicure, footwear and being absolutely clean enhances one's personality and helps you to become an achiever in life.

If you are basically shy and diffident, you may not be able to have a look of confidence on your face or carry yourself confidently that will impress people. If you walk with a feeling of failure and frustration your face and postures will reflect it and people will keep away from you. The way you walk, sit, talk or eat leaves an impact on the people around you and having a confident body language can do wonders for your personality. Walk in an upright position with shoulders straight. Do not droop. Sit erect and adopt a relaxed posture while conversing with people taking care to make eye contact.

If a confident look doesn't come naturally to you, act confident. It's not difficult to hold your head up, draw your shoulders, stand and walk upright and move more briskly. When you keep practising these for long, it becomes a habit and you will become more confident.

With people spending more and more time in front of TV and computers they have less real-life social interaction and lose their social skills and chances to develop their personality.

See what Vincent Nichols says: "We're losing social skills, the human interaction skills, how to read a person's mood, to read their body language, how to be patient until the moment is right to make or press a point. Too much exclusive use of electronic information dehumanizes what is a very very important part of community life and living together."

Chapter-16

Body language and courtship

"She is a woman, therefore may be wooed; she is a woman, therefore may be won."

—Shakespeare

*I*f you are in love your body will demonstrate it. Some courtship signs are studied and deliberate while many are unconscious. Body language of love, like its general aspects, is mostly inborn. But there are many that can be cultivated by conscious and consistent attempts.

When a person enters the company of the opposite sex, certain physiological changes take place unconsciously.

When a man and a woman meet: If the man is interested, he will assume an erect posture, pull stomach in, hold head high and try to become more youthful-looking. A woman, who is interested, will emphasize her breasts, tilt her head, and expose her wrists and make herself more submissive.

Women initiate

All studies into flirtatious encounters show that women are initiators most of the time. The woman sends a series of subtle eye, body and facial signals to the targeted man. Very often men ignore these cues and simply walk on without responding to her signals. But on the other hand, very often men misinterpret friendliness and smiling for sexual interest and approach them from this angle to be denied by women.

Human courtship steps

Courtship usually takes place in a predictable 5-steps-pattern which is enumerated here.

Eye-contact: When she spots the man she fancies, she sends her gaze towards him. It takes several attempts to gain his attention and when he notices, she looks into his eyes for about 5 seconds and then looks away. After a few minutes she searches for him and gazes at him, their eyes meet again; this is the start of the flirting process.

Smiling: When their eyes have thus met a few times, the woman gives a fleeting smile for the man to take the initiative to approach her.

Preening: If a woman is attracted to a man she will start playing with her hair for 5-6 seconds to show she is grooming for her male. She may lick her lips, straighten clothing and jewelry. Man responds by standing straight, pulling his stomach in and expanding his chest, adjust clothing, touching hair and tuck his thumb into the belt or trousers. They point their entire bodies to each other showing mutual attraction and liking.

He approaches to have a casual talk: The man in question, if he can muster enough courage normally approaches the girl/woman to make a casual talk and get introduced. He may ask her name and other whereabouts. She will enquire about him too.

Touch-stage: When they meet again, if her fancy towards him is still strong, she looks for an opportunity to make a slight touch on his arm either accidental or otherwise. They may shake hands. This can be a quick way to the touch stage.

When a woman is with a guy she likes, she will touch, fondle and play with her hair and its braids. She will also adjust her clothing in an attempt to make herself appear better. She will also flick her head back and toss her hair over her shoulders. This bares her backside neck and her soft wrists.

Fondling a cylindrical object such as her finger, the stem of a wine glass, an earring, keys—anything similar or taking a ring from the finger and putting it back indicates strong interest in the man. If she does these repeatedly, she has definite unconscious sex craving. More sensual women may stroke her neck and throat. If she is seated she will tuck one leg under the other that points to the man she has found interesting. If they are seated across a table, she will place one hand on top of the other to support her face and to present it to him as if it was on a platter for him to admire.

Hand bag: When seated a woman may place her handbag close to the man she likes and will fondle it too as they talk or simply sit relaxed. A romantic woman will expose the smooth, soft underside of her wrists often to the man beside.

Signs of non-interest: Crossed arms across chest or a hand bag held against chest indicate she is not interested. If a woman tries to lean or move back from the man who has invaded her personal space, tells the man to keep away. If the woman likes the man she will have long eye-contact, her face will become radiant and she will come nearer as they sit and enjoy the company of the two. If on the other hand, she tries to keep a distance, is looking away from him or if her feet are held not pointing towards him—all show disinterestedness.

A man should not approach a woman from behind but meet her from the front. And eventually angle himself to 45 degrees. A man will use his protruding thumb from belt or pants to show interest in the woman nearby. Thumbs tucked into the pants or belts shows an aggressive sexual attitude.

Men should avoid crotch adjustment when in the company of women.

The way you look/appear affects your ability to attract and keep a partner.

People we meet form about 90% of their opinion in just 4 minutes and our physical desirability is assessed in less than 20 seconds. Both men's and women's brains are wired to be attracted to those who show most physical prowess and reproductive ability. You don't have to be handsome in the traditional sense to attract good looking people from the opposite sex. But you have to be physically fit and healthy and radiate warmth and strength. As a general rule, we all look for those who are more or less as attractive as we are. There is always a fear lurking inside whether a more desirable one will steal our chosen one.

Signs of consolidating romance

Extended eye contact: The more we are looking at someone the more interested we are in them. **Touching the hand, elbow, hugging good-bye for longer** than necessary, are signs that both are falling in serious love. **Body directions.** A man will point his feet and body towards the woman he has taken a fancy in and he will try to close the space between them. Her body and feet will be turned towards him too and she will be eager to be nearer to him physically and emotionally.

How to understand your romance is breaking up?

- Covering ears or putting a finger into the ears show he/she is lying about the relationship.
- Rubbing eyes vigorously is also one signal. Women will use small and gentle touching motions below the eyes.
- A rub or a scratch at the neck tissue will indicate the same too.
- If he/she scratches nose or neck tissue while speaking he/she is probably lying.
- Trying to block words or covering mouth while speaking show that what he/she is relating isn't the truth.
- If one of the partner's eyes is darting here and there instead of extending eye-contact, he/she is looking for escape routes.
- If their feet and body are pointing towards other directions, they are breaking the newly-found romance.

- People who are feigning affection will repeatedly tap your shoulders.
- Extended blinking in any partner is a sign of disinterest.
- If men and women sit with ankle locks it is reasonable to assume they won't be seeing each other again.

Ways to become more attractive to the opposite sex

Research shows that both men women can become more sexually attractive by taking care of a few things on a day-to-day basis.

- Taking care of personal hygiene–shower perhaps twice–morning and evening.
- Trim your hair, beard, pedicure, manicure and let your body be absolutely immaculate.
- High status clothing is universally admired—both by men and women. May be you can go in for branded well-tailored well-fitting modern clothes. Women look for class.
- Women should apply make-up 'use high heels, bright red lip stick and emphasize their cleavage.
- Contact lens will make women's eyes more attractive.
- The more you smile the more positive reactions others will give and the more attractive you will seem.
- It is good if men learn to dance.
- Men should avoid putting their hands in their pockets.
- Women love men who can make them laugh. And men love those who laugh at their jokes.
- Confident and open body language is helpful for all.
- Smiling enhances attractiveness and that a smile is interpreted to be a signal of a woman's interest towards a man.

Courtship is a fundamental requirement of human life. Each one of you –man or woman – must have a partner worth you. Whatever effort called for is worth it. But unless and until you have a good personality you won't be attracted to a worthy individual you deserve. Let these pages help you a little to make you more confident and attractive.

Chapter-17

Meet new people

"Walking with a friend in the dark is better than walking alone in the light."

—Helen Keller

Meeting new and different kinds of people is a healthy step towards expanding your horizons and exposing yourself to a larger number of things. You get an opportunity to know more about other cultures and lifestyles and it significantly has a positive effect on your own personality.

We all know how important friends are. Having a best friend is a huge bonus in life. He/she offers you comfort, chases away your loneliness, gives unconditional support, boosts your self-esteem and gives you honest opinions. Good friendship yields a multitude of long-term physical and emotional health benefits. Studies show that healthy relationships make aging more enjoyable, lessen grief, and help you reach personal goals.

When you meet new people, you are expanding your network. Whether you are in a new town or city you look for new personal or professional connections. Meeting new people can impact various areas of your life and help in many crisis. **Renowned scientists Christakis and Fowler** present compelling evidence for the profound influence on one another's tastes, health, wealth, happiness, beliefs and even weight. *The advice is stay connected: there is a surprising power for our social Networks.*

Meeting new people and making new friends is hard for many of us. We're all busy, and it's not easy to just come across people with similar interests.

Once we are out of college or university we don't have avenues to find new friends and we don't normally try to get them. It takes more time and work. It can be difficult to meet new people; sometimes, you might feel like you have to repress or modify your personality a bit. The older we get, the more difficult it becomes to meet new people.

Making friends doesn't need to be complicated; often you can meet new people just by changing a few things in your daily routine. The trick is to get interested in others, chat or do small talk with those you meet anywhere—at the church or temple, at the library or cinema halls, at the sports event, at the milk booth or grocery, at the bank, stadium or even at the supermarket.

The end of a friendship can sometimes come unexpectedly and it can be painful too. New friends can fill the void and make you cheerful again.

If you're anxious where and how to meet new people, the following may help you out:

If you're desperate for friends, you may not make good choices. **Go about it casually**—relaxed without much conscious efforts. Friendship should spring and bloom effortlessly and naturally. You start noticing things about people, becoming polite and making connections. Seeing them like this is a good way to start up a conversation and get to know them better. It's somewhere where the situation breaks the ice naturally giving people reasons to talk to each other. It should be spontaneous. When you see the same people several times you get a chance to get comfortable with them and gradually get to know them. There is no point if you have one five minute conversation, make a good impression and then you never meet again. Keep in touch with them, visit each other and develop a healthy friendship.

Pull a conversation from the setting: If you are watching a cricket match with strangers, talk about the game, how a move has faltered, where a strike has been exemplary, your companion may simply agree with your observations and it leads you to further small talks. If you are standing in a line you may open up something relevant about the place or about a burning political issue.

Get into something new

Perhaps the best way to meet new friends is to go in for something new. It can be a new hobby, taking a class or course where there will be many others enabling you to connect with someone you probably would never have crossed paths before with. A new course or project will automatically help you as it gives out a vibe saying you're open to learning and conversation, which is the perfect way to start a new friendship.

Strike a conversation with those you meet regularly

You can try to enter into a conversation with those standing in your queue on a regular basis. Church or temple is a perfect setting for new friendships to bloom.

Internet: It's amazing how the Internet has become, in the last few years, a great place to make friendship. The Internet can help introduce you to people through Facebook, Linked-in, Twitter, Whatsapp and others. Many of them will become your friends at some point. We all spend so much time in front of the computer that it makes sense to start new acquaintances. A few years ago, there was no venue like this. This is perfect even for introverts as you don't have to meet anyone physically. You are in a virtual world exchanging greetings, ideas, wishes, opinions paving the way for later friendship. There are millions of websites and other platforms for people to communicate and connect through media that are all over the Internet these days.

During travel

If you're shy and withdrawn, striking new friendship during travel will be a daunting task. But during a long boring train journey, there is ample amount of opportunity to casually enter into a conversation, get to know each other and develop a bond.

Book group or literary club

If you love books there are several ways to connect with new people. You may join a literary club or a book group. Anyone can enjoy a conversation about literature or politics. The great part about joining one of these groups is that you'll meet a variety of people.

In your workplace

You can easily make friends at the workplace. It's easy to get to know the people you spend at least eight hours a day with. Apart from the regular staff, there are so many others who come to the office –vendors, salesmen, customers, consultants, and you will be, as apart of your job, talking to them. Someone may appeal to your nature; get interested in them and may be a friendship would bloom.

Gym

If you're looking for new friends, gym is a good place to find them. Join one and take a few exercise classes. Another way is to look for a group run or walk in your neighbourhood or town. Join them and meet people with similar interests.

Revive an old friendship

Why not try to revive some of your past friendships? You can learn a lot about your school or college mates, teachers, seniors and juniors and many others. One or two old friendships might be worth starting up again. Sometimes friends just drift apart as you get a job, marry and start with a family or begin to have nothing in common. But all that can change when you establish contact again. It will be a pleasant experience too.

Become a volunteer

Volunteering is a good thing to do to help build your self-esteem. It gives you chances to connect with others. Why not make friends while you help someone else? You'll meet passionate people who can show you a different side of things. There are so many social organizations looking for volunteers.

Break your routine

You may have to force yourself out of your routine to meet new people. If you are struck in your daily life pattern, work-home-computer and TV you will not be able to meet new people—you have to come out of it and try new ways: add social hobbies, come out of your home or comfort zones and go for a walk or to a movie.

Join a social club

There are many of them that you can find in any town. Rotary, Lions, Wise-Men's, Toastmasters are international social organizations. There are many local and country, aquatic, and social clubs and gymkhanas. There are family and spinsters groups too to choose from.

Don't get discouraged: You may go to a few social events and not really run into anyone you could strike a friendship with. The whole thing can be done but is elusive. Then you join a club and instantly and effortlessly you make a group of good friends. So don't get discouraged if your first few attempts don't bear any fruit. You'll meet some new friends easily through a handful of avenues, while other ones won't really work for you at all. For example, someone may start dancing classes and feel there's plenty of opportunity to get to know many new people as they are always coming and going. But at last nothing worked.

It's not enough just to have many friends; good friends should nurture you and help you to grow into a happy and successful person. If you have a lot of friends, but don't feel fulfilled emotionally, perhaps you haven't met the right ones who can help you feel comfortable. Don't be afraid to get out and meet more new friends, because some of them might unexpectedly change your life for the better. You opt to meet people who are similar to you, in terms of your hobbies, goals and values. New people are continually entering your life from all quarters. There comes a time when you may have a lot of friends in your life, which is certainly a blessing.

You are the most important person in your life. You live your life as yourself and try to treat another as you would like others to treat you. You treat another as the most important person. Appreciate the inner beauty of every person you meet. You can smile and everyone around you knows that you are happy to be with him or her. Smiling is infectious when you smile the other person smiles too.

Let us keep an open mind and leave our prejudices away. You don't try to defend your beliefs and mistakes. It's very easy to tell the other person 'you are wrong.' You yourself can be at the wrong side, but you don't recognize it and you blame the other. Be open for new ideas and look at things more objectively. Each one of us perceives things the way we are— according to our map-beliefs and prejudices. Your past conditioning makes you immediately judge others and pass comments without taking care to study people objectively.

We instinctively like certain persons and dislike others at first sight. We should become aware of this. How we behave to people will very much depend on the impression they create on us at first sight. That is purely subjective; no effort has been done to assess the individual objectively. The first unconscious feeling you get when you meet someone can be totally deceptive.

Most of us are interested in ourselves and hence we talk about us most of the time. If a conversation is going in a particular direction, we will direct it in such a way as to include ourselves in it. A magical dimension happens when you begin to give priority to others. Being a good listener could be a first step. And talking less is another. Try to understand the state of mind of the communicator. Grasp fully what the other person is saying. Do not interrupt; do not complete a sentence of the other. Sometimes people just want to be heard, they long for attention.

In any conversation we tend to judge others. We label others and constantly judge whether that is good, bad, ugly or awful. When you meet a guy you immediately 'judge,' 'oh this guy isn't good;' but what do you know about him to make that judgement? Your instant impression? Haven't you heard 'don't judge a book by its cover? Most of your judgements will be incorrect.

When you judge you are colouring your perception. You are blocking any further improvement of the person's image. This is gong to stick in your mind and will influence your later dealings with him. You are put into a prejudiced mind. We need to control the thoughts that creep in from nowhere as we meet someone and be patient to form an opinion.

Don't argue: I have heard that an argument is the best way to make enemies. By arguing you can never perhaps convince another. More often it ends in a fight or resentment. People normally tend to stick to their point of view. Even if they are convinced, they don't admit. *Argument is like a double edged sword.* It hurts you and it hurts the other. If one loses he feels sad, and he resents it. None gains anything from an argument. We all have an intrinsic feeling that what we feel right is to be appreciated. But each one of us feels differently about the same thing and hence arguments are bound to happen unless we control ourselves. Decide not to argue; you are not going to gain anything out of it and you will end up spending a lot of your energy.

Learn to see things from the other person's point of view. Each one is different—genetically, physically and mentally. Heredity and childhood experiences that make up your personality are totally different from another's. You believe in a religion while another may not believe in a god at all. You may be supporting a political party when the other follows a totally different one. What you believe is totally true for you and you will argue for them. You don't think the other person has the right to consider his beliefs to be true too. See things from the other person's shoes will obviate arguments and make friendship bloom.

"One of the most beautiful qualities of true friendship is to understand and to be understood."

—Lucius Annaeus Seneca

Chapter-18

Etiquette and manners

"The first rule of etiquette a boy learns when he's about to enter society is that civility is due to all women. No provocation, no matter how unjust and rudely delivered, can validate a man who fails to treat a woman with anything less than utmost courtesy."

—Ilona Andrews

Social behaviour has unwritten but universally accepted norms and ways. Etiquette is nothing more than a system of getting well with people socially. Those who succeed in life usually are well-mannered. The rules have evolved with man's social evolution. Cheerfulness and good manner always go together.

We shall begin our discussion with **Table Manners.**

Eating is a social activity common in all lands. Since we eat in groups, if the other fellow's table manners is sloppy and disgusting, eating will be a bad experience. The material you use for serving is immaterial. The simplest meal will be more enjoyable if all follow good table manners.

- After seating at the table unfold the napkin and place it across your knees. Don't shake it out, tuck it under your collar, belt or around your neck. It is for rubbing your lips, wiping your fingers, and protecting your lap from dropped food. After the meal, place it folded beside your plate.

Forks are always placed to the left of the service plate, and spoons and knives to the right. The cocktail spoon or fork is generally placed on a small plate holding the cocktail. A spoon can be used for fruit cocktail and after using the spoon lay it on the plate beside the cocktail glass.

- Knife is used to cut and butter bread, or cut things like meat or chicken. When you do not use a knife, keep it across the upper edge of your plate with its cutting edge towards the centre. Do not use it for putting food in your mouth or place it with the tip on the plate and the handle on the table cloth. It might slip. When you cut meat, cut only one or two bites at a time. Lay your knife down, eat these, and then cut more.

A plate littered with small pieces of meat and vegetables doesn't look nice. Keep all your food on your service plate in separate sections to make it look more organized.

- Food is placed into the mouth with the fork and never with the spoon or knife. The fork can be held in the right or left hand. When not in use, keep it in the plate with its handle at the edge. When you are through, place the spoon and fork together, handles on the right edge of the plate.

Spoon is used for soup, fruit-cocktails, coffee, liquid deserts. A good rule is never to eat food with spoon that can be eaten with a fork. Do not bite from a whole slice of bread or toast. You can butter vegetable and potatoes with the fork. Some things which cannot be eaten with a fork or spoon can be eaten with fingers: olives, celery, small green onions, pickle, potato chips, bread and butter, rolls, and in some places fried chicken. Eat fruit with your fingers if they are sliced up and forks are not provided.

If you are shown a small bowl with water after a meal, dip your fingers into it and dry them up with your napkin.

While eating soup, dip the spoon away from you and towards the centre of the soup bowl, and drink it out of the side and not from the front of the spoon. Do this without making sound. Eat asparagus and French fried potatoes, pie and cake with a fork. If you eat a cake with hand, break a small piece and eat before taking another. Ice cream is generally eaten with a spoon.

- After putting cream or sugar in your coffee or tea, stir it gently with your spoon. Then remove the spoon lay it in the saucer and drink your coffee from the cup. Drinking from the saucer is not allowed.

When there is a lady with you in a formal dinner, go in quietly with the others wait for the hostess to tell you where to sit and let the lady sit first by pulling out the chair for her. Sit quietly at the table with your hands in your lap until the hostess begin to eat. Do not grab spoon or fork and play with them. Eat slowly taking time, talk to the next person in a low voice and you cannot shout across at another seated far away. Hold your elbows close to your body. A little practise will teach you how to use knife and cut the toughest steak without bumping into your neighbour. Don't rest your elbows on the table when you eat. When a dish is passed help yourself and pass it. Don't shout for anything; let the bearer come to you. Try not to spill the food on the floor, table or clothes.

In a buffet lunch stand politely in the queue, take carefully a little of what you want in the plate without letting food fall down and keep the ladles in their proper place. Go to a table with your food, get yourself seated properly and start eating as mentioned above.

Keep your mouth closed while eating

Chewing with your mouth open, making some ugly sounds or talking with food in your mouth are ugly manners. Keep your lips closed while eating and talk only after gulping down the food in the mouth. Otherwise you will spill food particles on to those you talk to. It is disgusting to see someone eat with mouth open and talk with others with food inside his mouth. When you have finished eating, remain at the table until the host or hostess rises to leave. If there is a lady on your right, draw back her chair as she rises and hold it apart for her to step out.

- When you go to a restaurant with a lady, the waiter will lead you to your table. Seat the lady first by pulling the chair for her. If there are two ladies seat both of them, the elder first before you seat yourself. It is nice if you can give both orders to the waiter together. No matter where you are dining, take your time, be neat and quiet.
- If you cough or sneeze, hold your napkin before your mouth and turn your head away from the table. You can leave the table after saying 'excuse me' to the person seated next and quietly return.
- Don't be late for any party. Speak to your hostess when you arrive, and concentrate on others there, never do or say anything that might offend others. If there is a lady who comes to meet you, shake hands only if she wants to. Wait for her to put her hand for you.
    - *Always stand for an introduction.*
    - *Give a warm and firm handshake.*
    - *Always mention names when you make an introduction.*
    - *Always introduce a man to a woman.*
    - *Look squarely at the person you meet and let your glance be firm but friendly.*
    - *When you speak with others, learn to be a good listener.*
    - *Introduce yourself when necessary.*
    - *Do not interrupt while another person is speaking.*

- *Talk about pleasant things and do not gossip or criticize.*
- *Always speak in a low voice and never shout.*
- *Do not shout across at others for any reason.*
- *Keep yourself under control all the time.*
- *You need to be friendly and helpful to others too.*

Remember it is ladies first when you are introducing others, sitting down at a table, going into an automobile, entering or leaving a restaurant. Hold the doors open for ladies wherever and whenever applicable.

Appearance talks

First thing strangers notice about anyone is the way he/she is dressed up and groomed. It may not matter how expensive the clothes are but how well-chosen, how well-fitting, how neat, how well-pressed and how suited they are for you and for the occasion do matter a lot. Shades of white for shirts and black/ blue for pants are Ok for office.

Grey and blue shades might be OK for suites for formal occasions. Shine and polish your shoes whenever you move out. Let your pockets not bulge with things inside them. You cannot wear shorts and T shirts to your office nor splashy coloured outfits. Leave your casuals for home/picnics. Gym and sports require exercise clothes and sports shoes.

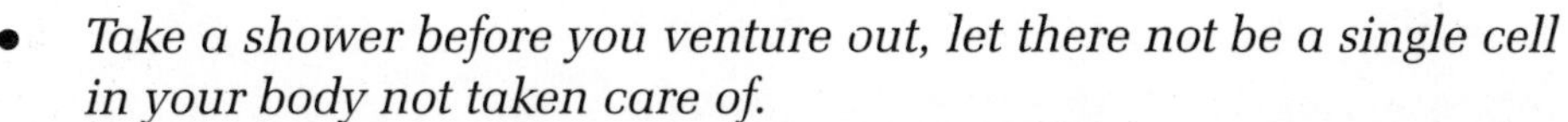

- *Take a shower before you venture out, let there not be a single cell in your body not taken care of.*
- *Brush your teeth and let them shine. If they are dull or dark a dentist can help.*
- *Cut your finger and toe-nails every week.*
- *Trim your moustache or your beard and comb your hair in the best way.*
- *Apply perfume which is soft and nice.*
- *Women can take some time for makeup, lipstick 'tilak' and 'sindhooram.'*

How you present yourself will very much depend upon how much care you have taken in your personal attire and grooming.

Next to appearance your manners are your best personal advertising. Let's try to be polite, punctual, disciplined and modest in drinks and eating. One has to follow etiquette everywhere—while eating, at the restaurant, in workplace or in a place of worship. You cannot be arrogant to anybody however low his position is. Politeness and friendliness go a long way in winning people's mind and hearts. With bad habits you may become a sheer nuisance to others.

- Being courteous is well appreciated and respected by all. Be humble and greet everyone with a smile. Never shy away from helping or supporting your colleagues and try to be available to them whenever they need you. Random acts of kindness will make somebody else's day and project you as a good person. Also it will give your personality a confidence boost.

You have to take an appointment while entering the office of a superior, you will behave in a funeral or marriage as per the customs of the people's sect or religion. There is office etiquette and written rules of behaviour for each corporation. You will behave appropriately in an office you visit. You will have to become a gentleman or lady in all spheres of life so as to get the appreciation of your superiors and colleagues and friends. Remember to give and take respect. It never hurts to be polite.

Chapter-19

Celebrate life

"Each day holds a surprise. But only if we expect it can we see, hear, or feel it when it comes to us. Let's not be afraid to receive each day's surprise, whether it comes to us as sorrow or as joy. It will open a new place in our hearts, a place where we can welcome new friends and celebrate more fully our shared humanity."

—Henri Nouwen

You have a very short life. On an average, 80 odd years after which there is going to be a veil of eternal darkness whether you like it or not. Hence live every minute, savour every moment. Let every second become a beautiful experience. There can be worries, there can be looming problems. But at this moment, you have the power to be happy or unhappy.

If you feel moody go to your favourite beach; let the sun and the fragrant wind soothe your nerves. Plan and go for a trip for tomorrow or the day after. Plan to take your kids for a movie or to an amusement park or anywhere they would be happy. Buy new clothes for your family members, buy the best automobile, go to the best restaurants for a dinner together; enjoy living.

As Oprah Winfrey has observed, the more you praise and celebrate your life, the more there is in life to celebrate.

Are you worried about money? If you have it why should you hoard it? Spend it and enjoy this day which will never return. And when you spend you feel like making more of it. Use your time and mind to make adequate money for your wants in life.

You might be sitting irritated over something when your child comes with a demand or childish prank. You will tend to get angry and spoil his/her day. Once an angry word has passed your mouth it can never be retrieved.

It would have caused an irreparable harm. The child goes unhappy grumbling and you become unhappy too. Why do you want to make a moment unpleasant? Hold your reaction for a minute suppressing the natural bend of mind to be angry; say a nice word, and offer a smile. If you are doing something, stop doing it and lend your ears and eyes, lend your body, lend your mind. The attentions you give will make all the difference in the world to your child.

When an aged parent comes to your side, do not feel irritated. Show warmth and concern. After all they gave all their time to you when you were young. They are the same parents now, the only difference is that they are no longer earning and they are not physically fit as they used to be. Your annoyance and eagerness to get rid of them will make them unhappy and if such events get repeated they will stop coming to you for anything. They will become more morose and lonely and they will start cursing their life and think of putting an end to it. In turn, knowingly or unknowingly you will feel sad and guilty. Everyone knows a feeling of hurt or guilt is very damaging to one's body and mind. If, on the other hand, you make them happy with your time and attention you will feel fulfilment. Enjoy your time with your aged parents, and if you are lucky to still have grandparents, spend time and celebrate life with them while you can.

This world is full of good and beautiful things. Those balancing rocks, gurgling rivulets, greeneries, fragrant blooms, tranquil lakes, and the whole beauty of this nature has been specially set for you. Things happen here so very naturally and in perfect harmony. See how the moon rounds the earth, the earth and the moon round the sun which along with all its planets and satellites rounds the galactic nucleus in absolute precision and harmony. A small seed germinates with tender shoots and grow into a big and beautiful tree. There is harmony and beauty in the birth of a child, the blooming of a bud and the downward meandering flow of a stream. All these have been going on here so very naturally for billions of years!

In any failure—however deep and painful— there are hidden elements of success and brilliant rays to guide and lead us up to light. Behind any deed there is a good intention. There are streaks of goodness in everything. Anyone can be happy at any moment. Our enemies are those whom we see as enemies. If we hate someone he will hate us back. If we love someone he will love us back too.

"We all have life storms, and when we get the rough times and we recover from them, we should celebrate that we got through it. No matter how bad it may seem, there's always something beautiful that you can find," Mattie Stepanek.

Let us celebrate this life. We are so very lucky to have taken birth in this universe during this advanced epoch. We are emanating from and going back into this universe. Little bundles of energy gave birth to us and they will return to the universal store house to live forever. We have no death; we will always live. Let us celebrate each second of the small time we have been allotted down here as humans.

Let us be grateful to our parents who gave birth to us, to the teachers who led us to the world of knowledge, to all our relatives, neighbours and friends who have loved and made us happy. We have taken birth to enjoy every second. There is joy in every cell of a new born baby. Let us love all, be grateful to everything in this world and make our life a thing of joy. There are so many around us who try to make our life comfortable and meaningful: teachers, traffic policemen, firefighters, guards and so on. Let's be grateful to them too.

Enjoy perfect health

Every cell of a new born baby is pure like a dew drop. Its blood vessels are transparent like a clear glass. How does it then become sick later? Eating more fatty food stuff like red meat, fried items, burger, and pizza, more salt and sugary aerated drinks is one; non-exercise is the other. Children are not trained to eat fruits, peas, lentils, vegetables and nuts. Instead, they get ice creams, cold drinks and fast foods. All these with alcohol, drugs and smoking bring in a host of health problems.

Almost 90 per cent of all diseases are related to the lifestyle of man. If one takes more food, fat gets deposited on the walls of blood vessels or elsewhere. Overweight, non-exercise and the intake of more salt coupled with the genetic propensity leads to BP, diabetes, cholesterol and heart diseases. Excess food—even carbohydrates— get deposited as fat in the body. If you are overweight your heart has to pump more blood, lungs have to provide more oxygen to more cells; stomach, liver, pancreas intestines, blood vessels and all have to work more exhausting vital energy of organs and the entire system.

If a disorder sets in, every living thing has a natural ability to get well. If a bone is broken it will be joined--if the broken pieces are kept together to heal. Doctors simply keep the broken bones in position and plaster to ensure they do not get disturbed during the healing process. If a blood vessel is cut, blood clots to prevent blood loss and the spot gets OK without any outside help. If the cut is large the clotting may not work and hence the wound needs to be closed for the body to do the healing.

If an animal is sick, it does not eat (but drinks water) and rests completely until it is healed. If humans get sick, we do not fast, we do not take complete rest for natural healing to be effective and complete. The disease worsens and we approach a hospital or resort to medicine to get cured.

We have ways to get well always: Eat less, that too whole grains, vegetables including leafy ones and deep coloured fruits. Take less sugar and salt; avoid fast food and fired stuff, take at least 8-10 glasses of water daily. Do

aerobic, muscle building and flexibility exercises and meditate for 15 minutes. Keep your memory and brain exercised. Be purposefully engaged and, become grateful to the universe for this life and love your dear ones.

Problem is with you, not with the world

There is nothing in the brain when a child is born into the world. There is no knowledge, no prejudice, and no inclination. It is like an untilled land. One can direct or make use of it anyway one wants to. But through his five senses information flows in uninterrupted and he soon forms a world view. He creates a map through which he views this world and its people. If the map has been well-formed, he would see the world right; a distorted map would find problems with all. How one has been programmed to view this life and the people around will determine one's entire life. Any event will be seen through the colour of your map. A person with a good map would look for lessons in a failure and start scheming for another attempt. When faced with a problem a bad map would see the whole world crumbling all around with no ray of hope.

An ill formed person finds bad things. All people seem bad to him. A well-formed one sees a lot of good everywhere. Instead of trying to correct the world, one needs to correct his personality. If you want to like others, you have to first like yourself. If you have to appreciate others you have to have self-esteem. If you hate yourself or have a lot of diffidence, in all probability, you will be a fault finder and a problem creator. The problem is with you and not with the world. Change yourself and the world will change automatically. Stop saying these negative things about yourself. Look in the mirror and find something about you that's positive and celebrate that!

One need not cry over one's bad childhood, bad parents, bad neighbours, poverty, lack of education and the not-so-good-looks; you can succeed by changing your map and by controlling your thoughts. If one does not make use of his brain and does not change his map, he will be a failure regardless of the attributes he has. If one does not love himself, the whole world will look bad. One has to try to be a success by starting to love oneself and feel good.

"I'm a really, really optimistic and really, really positive person. My main thing is, Enjoy life. Celebrate life."

—Luke Bryan

Chapter-20

Effective communication

"Take advantage of every opportunity to practise your communication skills so that when important occasions arise, you will have the gift, the style, the sharpness, the clarity, and the emotions to affect other people."

—Jim Rohn

Effective communication skills are fundamental to a successful life. Many jobs require it and people with improved communication skills usually enjoy better relationships in general, at the work place and at home.

Effective communication helps us to understand a person or a situation better and enables us to resolve differences, build trust and respect. Much of what we try to communicate to others—and what others try to communicate to us—get misunderstood causing problems. By learning to communicate effectively, you can connect better with your spouse, kids, friends, boss, subordinates and co-workers.

*As **Tony Robbins** has mentioned, "To effectively communicate, we must realize that we are all different in the way we perceive the world and use this understanding as a guide to our communication with others.* Understanding others and the way they see the world and us is quite crucial in any meaningful communication."

In this advanced age, we have to send, receive, and process huge numbers of messages every day. You need to master verbal and non-verbal skills, attentive listening, the ability to recognize and understand your own emotions and those of the persons you're communicating with.

Communication is a two-way process so improving communication involves both the sender and the receiver.

- **The first rule is to think of what you say.** Do not simply blurt out what comes into your head; instead, take a moment to pay close attention to what you say and how you say it. If you observe politicians you will know they do not blurt out whatever that comes to their mind. They give thought to what they are going to say and how to present it. Words once gone out cannot be retrieved and the harm is already done.
- **Maintain a positive attitude and smile.** People do not want to be around someone who seems to be often miserable. Maintain a positive, cheerful attitude to life: even when things do not go as per your plan, stay optimistic and learn from your mistakes. If you smile often and stay cheerful, people are more likely to respond positively to you. Do not complain to others unless it is absolutely needed. People try to keep away from those who seem to have perennial problems.
- **A communication is more effective when it is done spontaneously rather than formally.** When you read what you want to say is less effective than when you speak off-hand from your mind.
- **Make sure you are heard properly and understood.** Choose an environment where it is right for you to communicate. Your listener should be attentive, devoid of stress and willing to listen. There should not be external disturbances too like noise and other adverse conditions.
- **You need to be an effective listener.** Focus fully on what is being spoken, do not interrupt while the other person is speaking and avoid being judgemental.
- **Listen to the other party even in a conflict.** Let them say how they feel. Wait until they are completely finished talking before you begin to speak. And do so in a calm, level voice. Don't yell or make accusations about the other party or their actions. Let them know you have heard their point and understood their view point. Sometimes, you have to agree to disagree and move on and you may not be able to have the last word. If one walks out do not go after him. Let him come back when he is calmer.
- **Avoid communication while you are stressed up.** If you are angry, you will not be able to control what you speak. When an emotion like frustration or anger overruns you, avoid communicating serious things.
- **Choose the right time and context.** Avoid discussions on serious topics in the late evenings –at the workplace- when people are tired or amidst a lot of noise. Choose mornings to conduct discussions about serious topics when people are alert, available, and more likely to respond with clarity.
- **Choose the right place, providing freedom for a two-way communication.** If you convey the news of a death or an accident,

you better don't do it while others are present. Do so in a private place. This will facilitate a dialog with a more mutual understanding and sharing of emotions.

- **Be crystal clear and straight to the point.** Avoid bombastic words, frills and legal language. Whatever message you say or convey through writing or orally is to be clear, precise and easily understood.
- Recognize and acknowledge the nodding and the 'I'm following your looks' from the listener.
- **Eye-contact:** It builds rapport, helps to convince people that you're trustworthy, and displays interest. During a conversation or presentation, it is important to look into the other person's eyes and maintain contact for a reasonable amount of time, not over doing it.

Body Language

We communicate more using non-verbal signals. Facial expressions, gestures, eye contact, posture, the tone of your voice; even your muscle tension and breathing convey a lot. The way you look, listen, move, and react to another person tells them more about how you're feeling than the words you speak. Understand and empathize with what is really troubling other people.

You can enhance effective communication by using open body language— hands open and held a little away from body, arms uncrossed, standing with an open stance, slightly leaning toward him/her while standing or sitting, relaxed and maintaining eye contact with the person you're talking to. Use voice modulation and avoid monotone and mono speed.

If you say one thing, but your body language says something else, your listener will likely feel you're being dishonest. For example, if you say you have been to USA a number of times (while you have not gone there at all) your body language will send signals that you are telling lies which the listeners will understand. When you speak the truth and what you believe, your body will make it convey better.

Communicating to a group

1. Organize and clarify ideas in your mind. This should be done before you attempt to communicate. Target at some key points to stick to when communicating, instead of beating around the bush. They will act as anchors helping you to focus and bring clarity to your

communication. A good thumb rule is to choose a few main points and keep your talk focused on those. If you wander, you will be able to return to one or more of these key points easily. Writing the points down, can greatly help too.

2. Don't lose track. Stay on topic. Once you start to convey make sure everything you say adds to the message you intend to communicate and strengthens it. If you have already thought about the message enough, it is likely that appropriate phrases will come out from you.
3. Avoid distraction of all sorts. It can be mobiles ringing, music from a set-anything that could interrupt the communication. Turn off anything that will distract both you and your listeners and will effectively kill the communication.
4. If you are presenting to a group of people, be sure to check the acoustics beforehand and practise projecting your voice clearly. Use a microphone if needed to ensure that your audience can hear you.
5. Make it clear what you are going to convey from the outset. Your purpose could be to inform others, obtain information, or initiate action. If people know in advance what you expect from the communication, things will be smoother.
6. Be articulate. It is important to deliver your message clearly and unambiguously so that the message is well- understood. Listeners should easily grasp what you say. Use simpler words instead of complex ones and short phrases and convey them distinctly.
7. Speak at a volume that is easy to be heard. Not too loud or in a low voice.
8. Modulate your voice, avoid monotone as it is not pleasing to the ear and do not speak at the same speed. Bring down the pitch when you appeal for an action. Raise the pitch and volume of your voice occasionally when you move from one topic to another. Increase your volume when you want to emphasize, and slow the delivery whenever you raise a special point or are summing up. If you don't employ principles of modulation your communication will be boring.
9. Take special care to properly stress the key points to avoid any kind of misunderstanding. Try to modify or polish your message by discussing with someone you can trust and is knowledgeable.
10. Be passionate on what you say and believe it. Then appropriate facial expressions, and body language and gestures will just flow in.
11. **There is power in pausing.** Experts say that pausing causes an audience to lean in and listen. It helps you to emphasize your points and allow the listener time to digest what has been said. It makes your communications more compelling and easier to absorb.
12. Thank your group for the time taken to listen and respond. No matter what has been the outcome of your communication, even if the response to the discussion has been other than what you had hoped, end it politely thanking everyone's input and time.

The meaning of communication is in the result. If your communication has not produced the desired result you have not in effect conveyed the information or communicated at all although you might think you have. If the feedback is the intended result the communication has been one hundred per cent successful.

If a politician speaks eloquently for hours and hours, he may not have communicated much to the audience who would be bored to the core. A simple guy would be very effective although he talks slowly and almost in a whisper. But people are in rapt attention and carry out whatever he wants. Gandhi communicated likewise. No eloquence, not much gestures and no public speaking technique. He talked from his heart whatever he believed and practised. He had clarity (avoided ambiguity), simplicity (neither difficult nor clothed in frills and fronds), precise and to the point.

Hence what you communicate would be highly effective if you follow these additional points.

The communicator must have absolute faith in what he communicates and he must be practising what he speaks. It should be true, precise, short, clear and to the point. What you speak should be audible and reach the intended person well. Being enthusiastic and passionate will help you assume appropriate body language, facial expression, and gestures. Employ proper diction, accent and pronunciation. Most of our communication is done in a nonverbal way–body language, facial expressions—looks, smile, postures, your energy level and gestures.

Words carry below 10% importance in any oral communication. Voice modulation has about 35% significance and body language more than 55%. What you want to convey is passed mostly non-verbally. Your body and face convey a lot. It is not the words you say but how you say them that helps to produce the intended result. We will enumerate here what affects your communication.

- How you are dressed and groomed will increase or decrease your confidence level and will directly impact what you have to convey.
- An upright posture—erect, shoulders drawn and head held high—and brisk movements convey energy and enthusiasm that help to register your communication.
- Keeping eye-contact and a pleasant facial expression is a very helpful.
- Preparation on what you have to convey improves your communication. Thorough preparation adds to your confidence levels too.
- Being highly knowledgeable on the subject helps improve your power and people will register what you have to say.
- Believing and practising what you say is perhaps the most important of the entire lot.

Preparation: Before any communication—let it be a written or oral communication to your boss, subordinates, colleagues, vendors or customers— plan your communication well going through the following steps. Walking straight into the office of your superior and blurting out whatever that comes to your mind will reveal you are not an efficient person and that you don't respect your boss's time. Even a report requires good preparation and vetting.

- Make a draft with all the points to be covered with facts and figures.
- Vet it for correctness and accuracy.
- Make it short, simple, clear and to the point.
- Edit to make it more attractive and impressive.
- Make a final draft. Your report is now ready.
- For oral communication, commit it to memory and go through it a few times to make sure you get the content in the set order when you actually deliver.

In an effective communication, the receiver understands the exact information that the sender intended and acts accordingly. While you instruct your subordinates, you can ask him to repeat what you said to make sure the message is understood as you want it.

What you say may not be what your receiver gets. Clarity, repetition of the main points and voice modulation will all help to get the message conveyed correctly. Many problems will occur in organizations if people fail to communicate properly leading to confusion and failure of targets.

"Wise men speak because they have something to say;
fools because they have to say something."

—Plato

Chapter-21

Say a big 'thank you'

"Thank you' is the best prayer that anyone could say... 'Thank you' expresses extreme gratitude, humility and understanding."

—Alice Walker

Today you live in peace. Think about the war times when lives were lost so easily, and when pain, suffering, and poverty were everywhere. Now you have your loved ones near you. Many had lost them in war, in natural calamities and in accidents. Today you live in an age of medical breakthroughs and communication revolution. You can talk to your dear ones abroad over the Skype instantly. In the past, remember, letters took months to arrive, if at all they did. Now you send an email and it gets delivered in seconds. Even kings in the past didn't have a fraction of the entertainment options you have today like the television, movie, electronic games, travels, adventure tourism, just to name a few.

Now you can update your knowledge in any subject as every knowledge is there on the net at home. Years before, you had to search it in an appropriate book in a library and a few centuries before, knowledge was transmitted orally; writing had not been invented yet.

You are blessed with friends, relatives, lover, partner, father, mother, grandparents, teachers, pets, house, garden, TV, computers, automobiles, aircrafts, ships, trains, fridge, job, health, food, entertainments, moon, stars, rainbow, sunset, sunrise, rain, snow, nature, animals, music, dance, night clubs, strangers and lots of love. There is really a lot to be thankful for. We are not aware of these and we take them for granted. Sometimes we need to experience a loss to appreciate the value of what we have. Become grateful for all you have this moment, this day.

A thankful heart is very important to our happiness and good personality. Enjoy the beauty, richness, love and opportunities that exist in life. Appreciate those who help us or give nice things to us.

Let us reframe painful or disappointing events as opportunities for doing something good. Let people who love you know that you are grateful to them. Be thankful for what you have as you never know when it will be gone.

As an anonymous poet has sung: *If your arteries have hardened and arthritis have slowed your gait, or if your dancing days are over, or if any other condition afflicts you, think of others with more pain like the fellow in the wheel chair or the one without hands or legs, and be grateful for the use of the right arm that can write a letter, for the eyes that can savour every flower, bird and tree, for the ears that can tune in the sounds they make and above all your brain, the greatest asset.* There are many who are mad, retarded or imbeciles who cannot use this wonderful faculty.

You cannot welcome more abundance into your life until you have said to the universe truly, "Hey, thanks for all I have". Place yourself in a better mood by being thankful. You will find you are in a much more optimistic state after you've spent a few minutes reflecting about your blessings and feeling grateful for them. Compassion and kindness will probably fill your heart.

Helen Keller was blind, deaf and mute; still she thought she was blessed and tried to cheer those who were blind.

Mark Ingles, whose legs were amputated below the knee in 1982 as they were frost-bitten while stuck in a snow cave for 13 days during mountaineering, feels there is a lot left to be thankful about. He is grateful he is alive and he conquered Mount Cook in 2002 and Mount Everest in 2006. And these days by travelling he inspires others to enjoy and appreciate this life.

If a person without both eyes, ears, vocal chords or both legs has so much to be happy about we sure can be happier and say a bigger thank you to this dear life and the universe which gave birth to us.

We are oblivious of our capabilities and forget what positive contribution we can make to our dear ones, our neighbours or to the society. **Everyone walking on this planet has some special ability hidden within.** Many of us do not attempt to bring it forth. **As Ruskin has put it,** *"The weakest among us has a gift, however seemingly trivial, which is peculiar to him and which if worthily used will also be a gift to his race."*

You have to identify this special gift. You have to know what you really love from an early age. Pursue the subject you enjoy, do what your mind likes. The tragedy starts when you do not follow these rules. Unhappiness results if you are engaged in something or live with someone you dislike. Or still, when you idle away your time doing nothing meaningful.

To feel really worthy be in an environment you love doing what you enjoy. Be healthy and vibrant: exercise, eat your cherished foods (in small quantities), hear selected songs and do not miss a chance to walk in the woods by the side of gurgling streams. Spending time alone in natural surroundings will mute your inner confusions and liberate your mind to see your special roles down these trodden ways. Converse with the universal intelligence and seek guidance. Read books of great minds and reflect on the eternal truths contained therein. Indulge in your special pleasures—whatever they are —without a prick of conscience. There is no sin in the world other than hurting a fellow traveller.

There is so much to be alive in this wonderful world and live it fully with a grateful heart. *Research shows that an attitude of gratitude bolsters your self-esteem, fights your negative emotions (like stress or anger) helps build meaningful social bonds, and releases endorphins in the brain that produces a sense of well-being.* Another university study shows that gratitude and thanks-giving can even increase physical health and longevity.

Look for opportunities to thank people. When someone does something for you— big or small—it's an opportunity to express thanks. They've made your life a little better than before. You will even start thinking that people try to make you happy. Thanking other people boost your own happiness and you feel valued and appreciated. As Simon Mainwaring has said, 'The simple act of saying thank you is a demonstration of gratitude.'

Start an attitude journal: Keep daily a list of events that you are grateful for each night. By focusing on the good things that came to you that day and how they planted fruitful seeds for a better tomorrow, you will get a feeling of succeeding with all the help coming to you. It removes a complaining mode from your mind and sets a best-outcome mindset.

When you're grateful to a lot of people and things around, you tend to share that contagious positive energy. People tend to be drawn to you. To achieve this, it's crucial to watch your words. You normally act what you say. Stop complaining about anything and replace the same with positive words and talk about your success and good things in life.

Life is a wonderful gift. **Make a list of ten reasons why it is great to be born in this century**. Make another list of ten reasons why it is good to be born in your family, as you.

There are so many things in your life you need to be thankful about. We simply take all good things—small and big— in life for granted. And we don't feel grateful for them! Express gratitude for your life, personality, IQ, education, job, home, parents, loved ones, neighbours, for being physically alright. Think about the illiterate paupers, think about the crippled, the blind, the deaf, the mute, think about the imbeciles, mad… you are so much to be grateful for.

Harbour no ill-feeling against anyone. If you lack something, no one else is responsible for it. Life is always a mixture—it does not come all the time in a silver platter.

"Develop an attitude of gratitude, and give thanks for everything that happens to you, knowing that every step forward is a step towards achieving something bigger and better than your current situation."

—Brian Tracy

Chapter-22

Develop a happy personality

Are you happy now? Well, that is all what really counts. The richest person on the earth— let it be Bill Gates, Warren Buffet, Carlos Slim or anyone else— they all want to be happy and peaceful every moment of their lives. We are here to be happy. Everything points to just these 9 letters arranged in this order: Happiness.

How can you be happy? This is the greatest of all questions. There are as many answers to it as there are those who think about it. When you attain a goal you are happy, even the journey is enjoyable. When you overcome your dirty habits you become happy. When you reduce your weight you are happy too. When you live with your dream partner you are happy. When you have lots of money you become happy. These are all things that will make you temporarily happy. When the cause of the happiness is taken away, you become unhappy again.

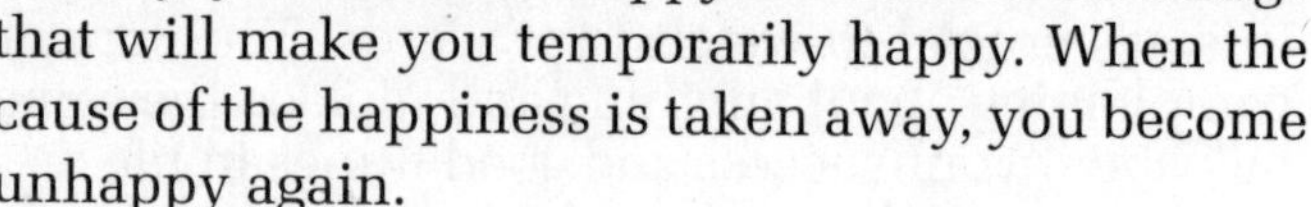

How can you be happy all the time? How can you feel an inner joy every moment? If you have wealth and a bad partner you might not be all that happy. If you become healthy, without enjoying the food you love, you will not be really happy. Even if you became the president of a company through years of hard work, you will not be happy if you do not enjoy what you do. If you do not know what to do with the wealth you have amassed you may not be happy again. You may be healthy, you may have an ideal partner but if you do not pursue your true calling, you cannot be happy too. We can have thousands of such permutations and combinations where you end up unhappy.

How can we be happy all the time and feel the fulfilment of having passed this way? Truly happy people would not exchange their life with anyone else's, however attractive the latter's may be. What can you do to become happy all the time?

- Make adequate money for your needs, and go with a steady job or engagement that you enjoy.
- Do not be crazy for more money or possessions. Simply appreciate and recognize what you already have.
- Know ways to reduce stress and anxiety and learn to reframe negative experiences.
- Develop a balanced worldview and do not become a slave to any religion or political party.
- Be happy that you have this wonderful life.
- Try to see bad things as temporary and good things as permanent.
- Be romantically involved with people of the opposite sex and have multiple close friendships.
- Try to resolve the problem you face then and there, instead of postponing to face them later.
- Feel free to do what you want and do not allow others to restrict you in any way.
- Avoid conflicts of all sorts with anyone— family member, neighbour, colleague, boss or subordinate.
- Be willing to cheer and help others.
- Try to be what you are, do what you like and get what you want.
- Enjoy whatever you have at the moment, live happily now and here.
- Try to be always engaged in a fruitful way all the time. Take up a job you enjoy and if the present one is not something you like change it for another you can love.
- You have to become fit and healthy.
- Do what you say and think. Thoughts and actions are to be in harmony.
- You have to take care of your dress and grooming.
- You should be able to remember things, names of people you meet and whatever you need to recall.
- Develop a grateful heart. Be thankful to the world and everyone around.
- Love your dear ones and try your level best to make them happy.

Live your lives!

Many of you may not be able to become immensely rich or famous, with great victories and glorious triumphs. But none of you is destined to wallow in misery or suffer throughout your life. None of you need to just pull on with your life by doing whatever little needed to get paid, feed your family, and pay the bills. But you can rank with those who simply enjoy living. You have the potential to live fully being happy, feeling fulfilled every moment.

But try not to adjust with a job you do not like, or with a partner you do not love, and spend your days knowing very well that you are not living your life. You have to live a wonderful life with a full blown positive personality.

You may have been leading a small life all the way convinced you are only capable that much and not more. Break these limiting beliefs! Live the life you enjoy, you are destined for. Do the job you love, find a partner you love and spend the free time the best way you want. Love those whom you like and get things in life you enjoy.

Get rid of worry

Many people waste their lives stuck in a state of constant worry. They worry about their children's poor grades, future, work, about the attitude of the boss, relationships with others, diseases, enemies, travel, the leak that has been developed in the roof… We worry about something now. When it eases off another worry crops up and when this one fades away a third is waiting to enter.

Worrying is a help if it makes you to take action, to solve a problem, avoid bad things or prepare you for the worst. But that rarely happens and mostly worry becomes a problem of its own. Some of us even worry about worrying too. Worry induces fears and sends one's anxiety levels soaring which interfere with one's day-to-day life. It is normally a habit and this can be overcome by training your brain to look at life from a better perspective. *The greatest comforting thought is that almost everyone worries– great leaders, painters, singers, authors, and the rich, the poor and all.*

I have heard about an old lady who worried all day long. But her real worry started by the sunset. She worried just about anything and everything and the funniest thing is that none of her worries ever materialized. **Studies done on worry show that more than 95 per cent of them never happen. And the remaining 5% will happen whether you worry or not. So why worry at all?**

Worry does not help tomorrow's problems in any way and the sad part is that it takes away today's happiness. When we worry about the future, we are destroying the future itself. Worrying does not help anyone; still, many find it hard to stop it. Worry comes uninvited and most of us feel it is not within our control to get away from this nagging problem. They rob you of the ability to laugh, love and share joy with your dear ones.

Is there no way to control worry or at least mitigate its debilitating effects? Constant worrying takes a heavy toll as it gives sleepless nights and makes your days edgy and confused. You may even believe that constant worrying will lead to diseases or that it may drive you crazy.

Well, if you sit and worry when it takes possession of your mind, it will bother you more and smother your faculties. Worrying rarely leads to solutions. You're no more prepared to deal with them should they actually happen no matter how much time you spend brooding over even in the worst case scenarios.

- *Distraction could be a way of escape.* Do something that can absorb you fully like engaging in your hobby, playing with your children, enjoying a warm bath, watching a hilarious movie, talking to someone you love, taking a walk in a quiet beautiful place, hearing a song you love, reading a book you cherished all along or playing your favourite game. But this is no permanent solution it will only lessen the tension worry induces.
- Remember telling yourself to stop worrying as it does not help in the long run. Your suppression of anxious thoughts makes them stronger and more persistent over a longer period.
- Why not assign a period for worrying every day? Half an hour you sit for 'worrying'. Follow the same place and time for worry: earmark say, 5.30 pm in the bedroom. During this 'worry period' you can worry about anything and everything but the rest of the day must be free of it. If worry thoughts prop up in between assign it for the worry time when you can indulge in it to your heart's content.
- Making a worry list for the worry time is found to be helpful too. Postponing worry helps as it breaks the habit of dwelling on any worry that props up then and there. Slowly you get more control on the worrying habit.
- Even deep, slow breathing and exhaling will calm you down and reduce the intensity of worry. While relaxed thus, focus on what you can do to solve the problem rather than what you cannot do.
- There is a very practical way to get rid of the tension from worry: relax your muscles. Take each limb of your body and hold it tight while you count up to 5. Release the tension and move it slowly sideways saying to yourself, relax, relax, relax. Start with your legs, then the buttocks, backside, neck, forehead, eyes, mouth, chest, stomach and hands. If you have relaxed each tissue in your body the tension induced by the worry would have melted away.

- Smiling is an anti-dot for worry too. Worry cannot reside in a person who keeps a smile. A good laugh is the medicine. If you frown, you worry more.

Thinking about all the things that could go wrong doesn't make life any more predictable or keep off bad things from happening. It is not possible to be certain about everything in the future. What is the need to be certain about? Let there be some uncertainty. Why should we predict bad things when the possibility for a bad occurrence is very low? Life is a short thing; let us be happy and enjoy this moment, next moment and the next. Always remember—

"*Past is history, future is mystry and present is the gift.*"

Chapter-23

Keep your memory strong

"An accurate and retentive memory is the basis of all success."

—Harry Loraine

*I*s your memory sharp and accurate? One Hundred per cent accuracy is only a dream. Do you think it is sharp enough and good enough that you can rely on it? Or do you think it is rather fading away? Only 20-25% feel that their memory is good. 35-40% feel their memory is poor. About 40% feel they have an average memory.

There is no good or bad memory. There is only trained and untrained memory, exercised or unexercised memory. Every memory is good. It becomes better with use and exercise and it gets rusted with disuse and neglect.

You remember better if you like a subject

It is true that we can remember more easily in the areas of our liking. If you are a singer you recollect songs easily. Students score higher in a particular subject because of his interest in it and less in another because of his lack of interest. I have heard them say, "I can't remember a thing of math. "But he will recall the stadium, city, country, year Sachin Tedulkar scored a century. He has a good memory in Cricket as he likes the game and is poor in math as he dislikes it.

Suppression

Memory suppresses what you do not like or what the subconscious mind has painful association with. We always recall the names of the people we like and forget the names of those we dislike. Mothers do not remember the details of the pain and labour of childbirth but vividly recall seeing and holding the baby with every detail. The latter made her happy and the former sad.

Impression

It is a major factor helping memorizing and recall. How deeply is the event or stimuli impressed upon the cells? Out of the millions of sight signals that reach our retina as we walk along a new road, a skyscraper is retained vividly. Its sheer size and height must have surprised you making you look again and again at different angles. The impression or image of the object gets thus indelibly marked. Whereas ordinary sights along the way is seen in a passing way and does not get impressed at all. Similarly, thousands of sound stimuli reach your brain but a few of them only gets recorded for recall. The shrill cries of a baby reverberate in your brain whenever you remember that journey. It caught your attention due to the high pitch, longer duration and the emotions it evoked in you. Its impression was stronger than that of a passing sound.

Repetition

Children remember and recall better what they study repeatedly. Repetitions make a better impression than reading once. Recalling something learnt at frequent intervals makes it indelibly marked in memory. If you give less attention to what you want to memorize, the weaker will be the impression and hence difficult to recall later.

Emotional interest boosts memory too

Normally learning a foreign language is difficult. But If you are told you are included in a trip to China and the people of the village you are going to visit speaks only Chinese, you will be immediately motivated to learn Chinese. Without interest nothing can be studied for retention, recall or later application. Interest can be evoked through motivation or excitement. Motivation is apt in the case of employees and excitement in the case of children.

A worthwhile goal and an intense desire to go up will help sharpen one's memory

In the absence of goals, people are drifting and they do not employ their mind or its powers. Things just come and go without leaving any mark. One who has fixed his goal and follows it, is on the move and will assimilate anything he finds useful on the way with full mind and emotional involvement and he will try to recall or apply them later on thus leaving a deeper impression in the memory cells.

Loss of memory

It may be true that the power of memory retention slows down with age. But as its power is very high and as we use only a fraction of it normally, this does not matter at all. Memory cells are lost if you bang your head against something or if you consume alcohol or drugs. An occasional loss of a few thousand cells of the brain may not affect you as there are over 100 billion neurons and as you do not use even 10 % of it.

If you exercise your mind and body and keep a thirst for life, you can recall, retain and memorize anything up to a good old age. But if you don't exercise your memory at all, it may have a premature death.

Do you think of sharpening your memory?

A strong memory depends on the health and vitality of your brain. There are lots of things you can do to improve your memory and mind. The human brain has an astonishing ability to adapt and change—even into old age. With the right prompting, your brain can form new neural pathways, alter existing connections, to improve its memory at any time. At any stage in life you can improve your cognitive abilities, learn new things and improve memory and recall.

- To start with, you need to have a nutrition rich and **healthy diet.** Eat more fruits, vegetables, whole grains, olive oil, nuts, fish and lean protein. Complex carbohydrates such as whole-wheat bread, brown rice, oatmeal, high-fibre cereals, lentils, and whole beans will help. Saturated fat from red meat, whole milk, butter, cheese, cream, and ice cream, etc. can increase your risk of dementia and impair concentration and memory.
- Do not deprive yourself of **sleep**. Research shows that sleep is necessary for memory consolidation, with the key memory-enhancing activity occurring during the deepest stages of sleep.
- Having enough **friends**, picnics to new places and enjoying humorous programmes do help activate your cells.
- Researchers have recently found that people with the most active social lives had the slowest rate of memory decline.
- **Laughter** is good medicine for memory too. Laugh more and enjoy humour from any quarter.
- Frequent or rather **daily mediation** improves focus, concentration, memory and learning ability. Stress, depression, anxiety, and chronic worrying can cause harm to your memory.
- Find out a **new activity** that requires using hand-eye coordination like knitting, or needle work, playing a musical instrument, juggling, table tennis, making pottery, and so on.
- Try to recall the details on either side of the route you took from the railway station to the place you went in a new city last week or a month before.
- Recall the synopsis of the book you read 6 months back. How much can you remember now?
- Try to recall the names of all your classmates in the 6th or 7th grades.
- In a **memory diary** write down the names of all people you met that day in the order of meeting. If your memory is dull already such a simple exercise will help if you do it for a year or so.
- Try to recall say 20 objects by connecting them in a series with ridiculous images. You can try to recall forward or backward with ease.

- Repeat the details what you discussed with a friend for a long time after 6 hours of the encounter.
- Play chess with different people and do different types of cross-word puzzles.
- Read the names of 25-20 objects once or twice with rapt attention. How many of them can you recall in the order in 1 attempt?
- Learn all the countries in the world using an atlas starting from anywhere and connecting each nation geographically. Say learn 10 countries a day. Repeat them from memory. After repeating them, add the next 10 nations and recall the 20 together and so on until you can say all the countries in any direction.
- Try to say the English alphabet in the reverse direction. In half an hour's times you will be able to do it.
- Recall a 12 digit number like 657903419238. It will become easy if you may make them into groups: 657, 903, 419, 238. Now study these numbers for one or two minutes. Close your eyes and recall them. If you get the whole number, great. If not, try to peg the whole in the memory by reading the whole number once more. Now recall again. In two or three more attempts, the entire number will be forthcoming. Now go reverse starting with the last digit first.
- Stop mentioning to anyone your memory is poor. No memory is poor. The moment you start feeling and telling yourself that your memory is good, it starts to function better. Your positive feeling and expressions are indirect commands to the brain, and if repeated often, they will produce positive results.
- If you know the date of each one of the first Sundays of the current year, (or look up in a calendar) it is easy to know the day of any date of the same year. Since there are 12 months there will be 12 first Sundays. Note down the dates of the first Sundays from January to December for 2015: 411537526416. Since the first Sunday of January is on 4th, 11th, 18th, and 25th are Sundays too. As 25th is a Sunday 26th will be a Monday and 27th a Tuesday. Memorize the number for the first Sundays by grouping them as shown: 411,537,526,416. What day will be the 8th of June 2015? If you recollect the above number, you will know that 7th June is a Sunday. 8th will be a Monday. What day will be December 25th, 2015? You will find that the first Sunday of December falls on 6th. Hence 13th, 20th are Sundays. 25th will be a Friday. Any day can thus be worked out from your memory.
- Physical exercise helps to sharpen your memory and brain. If you don't take care of your body, your mental faculties will suffer.

"Memory... is the diary that we all carry about with us."

—Oscar Wilde

Chapter-24

Avoid forgetfulness

"Your memory is a monster; you forget—it doesn't. It simply files things away. It keeps things for you, or hides things from you—and summons them to your recall with a will of its own. You think you have a memory; but it has you!"

—John Irving

You do not remember your mobile, keys, glasses, pen, CD, pen drive, IPod, shopping list, umbrella or something like that you kept somewhere a while ago. Or, you forget to take something when you go out or still, you forget to do something you had decided earlier.

Before retiring, a housewife locks her shelf and 'hides' the key so that a thief cannot find it. The next day morning she forgets where she hid it, and a long frantic search follows.

She locks her shelf that night and 'hides' it somewhere else (she thinks the thief knows where she hid it yesterday) and she goes through the same routine of a long, arduous search in the morning. This robs away her valuable time and causes a lot of irritation to her and to the rest of the family.

We all tend to forget many things when we go out, come off from the office or while we go shopping. Wives forget the place they kept the key the previous night; students forget what they learnt during exams and so on causing a lot of pain, irritation and other problems.

Is there not a way out?

- Assign a particular place for each of these objects you tend to forget on a regular basis and keep each file in a particular position in the rack. When you want any of them you would remember 'the place' and your hand would move towards it in a reflex action.

- Follow an order at home and office; let each and everything have its own place and do not allow them to be strewn around.
- Exercise your memory with memory games like crossword or logical puzzles regularly.
- To avoid forgetting things while you go out, link each one you need to take with the last door you would pass (mentally see the door carrying 'the thing' in a ridiculous way). Alternately, you may keep a list of the objects you have to take with you pasted on to the door. As you go out, the door would remind you about the items to be carried that day. The same technique can be resorted to while you come off from your office after the day's work.
- Make a shopping list before hand, commit it to memory by making them into a series with ridiculous connections and run through the list mentally once or twice before you go out. Leave the list at home and shop using memory. This is a good exercise to strengthen your memory.
- If you have the habit of forgetting to do something while you go out, link an image of it to a very popular landmark of the place you go to. You would be reminded of the thing to be done whenever you come across it.
- Students can recollect something studied a few times at intervals to recall it easily.

Remembering names

By remembering names, you are paying a subtle compliment and adding importance to the people you meet. Normally we tend to forget names and recall faces as visual images are retained better than auditory ones.

There are many silly techniques people use to show that they remember names. A leading politician used to ask those who came to meet him: 'How is that old sickness of yours?' The visitor gets impressed as he thinks the leader remembers everything about him. But who does not have an 'old sickness'? There are others who ask: what is your first name? (As if he knows the surname) This is only a trick and cannot be a substitute for remembering names.

To remember the name of a person

- Try to hear it properly. Usually you do not hear the name clearly nor allow it to get registered in your mind.
- Know how the name is pronounced and spelt.
- Know the surname and the expansion of the initials.
- For effective recollection repeat the name a few times as you speak to him/her.

- Take interest in him (try to know about his work, family and so on) and gather as much information as possible.
- Let each question begin with his name: 'Stephen, can you please tell me something about your people?' 'Stephen, where did you study?'
- Make sure you look at him and associate his name with the features of his countenance as you repeat them.
- Another technique is to associate the features with something you already know. This is not very easy. You may connect a particular feature of his face to the thing represented by the meaning of the name, if it has one. Later, whenever you see him you will notice the feature and the thing associated will come to your mind and the name will prop up from nowhere.
- Note down in a **'Memory Diary'**, the names of the people you met that day in the chronological order just before retiring. It will help strengthen your memory. You need to spend fifteen minutes or so each day before sleeping. Do this exercise and see the way your rusted memory revives enabling you to recall the names of the people you met.

Remembering names is very important to advance in one's social life, career and success. You have to remember thousands of names as you chart your course.

Chapter-25

Sleeping and personality

Just like eating, sleep is a necessary factor for the survival of all species. Proper sleep is required to be healthy, to maintain one's brain sharp and creative. Sleep gives our body enough rest and prepares us for the tasks ahead during the next day. It is like offering your body and mind a mini-vacation. Lack of sleep induces stress and loss of concentration. It leads to numerous health problems like hyper tension and suppressed immune system. It is also a reason for decreased ability for decision-making and math problem solving. Sleeplessness can make one eat more and thus augment weight-gain. Insomnia can lead to increased blood sugar level resulting in diabetes!

How many hours should one sleep? Some sleep 4 hours, others 8 and some on some days more than 10 hours! Opinions vary on the number of hours one should sleep. Very busy politicians sleep about 4-5 hours. There are those lazy guys who snore off for more than 12 hours too. Theories say enough sleep is important for compiling memories for transforming experiences and learning into improved performance. It could be safe to assume that in a 24-hour-cycle the human brain requires 8 hours of sleep. Sleeping 8 hours keeps your brain at the optimum efficiency; skin and body nourished and adds a few extra years to your life too.

There are mothers who spank the buttocks of their kids to wake up by half past five! These children must have had only about 6 hours sleep and they would doze off when they sit to read. **The deficient sleep accumulates in the brain** and whenever it gets an opportunity, the individual just dozes off. Adequate sleep is necessary for learning anything well.

There are so many who struggle in the bed to get to sleep. There are as many advices too. One story goes like this: count from 1 to 100 or more (until you sleep). One lady started counting and she reached thousand without any sign of sleep descending on her. Nevertheless she continued and reached 10,000. Still sleep eluded her and she was still counting when it was dawn! Getting proper sleep is rather simple if you follow some general guidelines.

Here are some tips:

- Develop a bio-clock so that your body gets programmed with a time for waking up, going to office, dinner....time for each and everything. Sleep every day more or less at the same time so that your brain automatically prepares you to sleep by around that hour.
- Do not engage in strenuous exercises a few hours before sleeping.
- Shut your mind off from all disturbing thoughts as you lie down. If you practise, your mind will shut off all worries and other disturbing thoughts as you lay down for sleeping.
- You can earmark a 'worry hour' for engaging in worry.
- Do not read exciting stuff or engage in hot discussions before going to sleep.
- If at all you want to read, do so something hard, less exciting or boring. Reading a detective novel for instance will keep you awake for long.
- Nothing should disturb you as you lie down, neither the sound of TV nor that of typing or conversations and loud shouts from the neighbours.
- It is good to take some sweet or a little honey before going to bed. Avoid strong tea or coffee just before sleeping.
- Eat at least 3 hours before you go to bed that too a light dinner. Your bedroom light should be subdued, and the bedding firm and comfortable.
- When you lie down leave everything aside and free your mind to sleep.
- Too much alcohol might send you to sleep immediately but the sleep will be short lived and not deep.
- Engage in half an hour's physical exertion (brisk walking, running or cycling with flexibility exercises) every day either in the morning or in the evening but at least 3-4 hours before sleeping.

If you follow the above points you would be able to sleep peacefully for a duration your bio-clock is accustomed to and you will be able to wake up fresh and recharged.

What your sleeping position tells about your personality

Each one sleeps in a particular way and it signifies a lot about you. Your sleeping position actually has a connection with your personality and the way you think, feel and behave. There's enough research to indicate that the posture adopted while sleeping has a lot to tell about you - introvert, confident, fun-loving, trusting, and so on.

Professor Chris Idzikowski, the director of the UK Sleep Assessment and Advisory Service, found most people don't change their sleeping positions throughout their lives. Lying down flat on stomach means better digestion, while those who lie on their back may end up snoring and breathing less well during the night.

Curled up on your side

This is the most common sleeping position, especially among women. According to surveys on the subject, those who sleep in the fetal position are found to be reserved, introvert and sensitive at heart although they appear sturdy and strong outwardly. They are reserved and they usually take time to open up to others but when they do, they are relaxed and comfortable. If you curl up into a ball like thing and you keep your knees to your chest, huddled together you're over protecting yourself. If you habitually curl up to your left side you may be experiencing increasing stress on your liver, heart, stomach and lungs. Therefore, curl up on the right side of your body.

Lying on your side with both arms straight down by your side

These people are found to be more sociable, even-tempered and they love to be with others. They are also very trusting with a tendency to believe anyone and hence they can get cheated easily. This position keeps the spine straight which is good for health.

Lying on your back with both arms at your sides

People who adopt this soldier sleeping position are found to be largely calm and aloof and they like keeping to themselves. They can be good task masters and set high standards for themselves and others.

Lying on your back with both arms up and around the pillow or sides of your head

These star-fish-pattern sleepers are found to be instantly likable people and great friends willing to listen to the problems of others and help those

in distress. If you have someone in your friends circle who sleeps likewise consider yourself fortunate. They don't like to be the centre of attention although they do become so very often.

Lying on your stomach with hands up and around the pillow and the head

Carefree people, they tend to shy away from absurd situations. They often appear to be confident, extroverted with enthusiasm and merry making attitude. But they are also found to be nervous and easily excitable and are sensitive to criticism. Any position in which you're lying face down is considered good in aiding digestion.

On your side with both arms out in the front

These people are easy going but cynical and suspicious and are open to new things. They yearn for something but set very high benchmarks for themselves. Slow decision makers by nature and weigh the pros and cons repeatedly. Once they make up their minds, they do not normally change the same.

Chapter-26

Keep a smile

*"People seldom notice old clothes if you wear a big smile." **—Lee Mildon***

"A smile is an inexpensive way to change your looks."
—Charles Gordy

A smile can set everything straight. It can dissolve another's anger, enmity or grudge. Even if someone is mad at you, you just smile without saying anything he will leave you alone. Give a stranger one of your smiles and it may be like a sunshine for him. Further, if you smile at someone, there is all possibility they might smile back at you too. Smiling is infectious; you start and set the chain going. *Always keep a smile on your face as a smiling face tells people that you are an outgoing and intelligent person worth getting to know.*

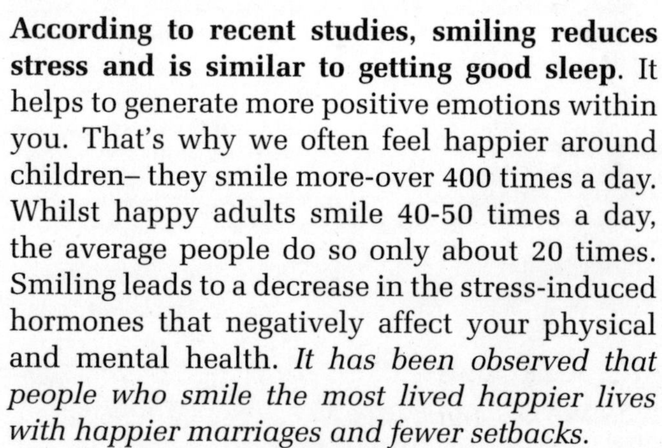

According to recent studies, smiling reduces stress and is similar to getting good sleep. It helps to generate more positive emotions within you. That's why we often feel happier around children– they smile more-over 400 times a day. Whilst happy adults smile 40-50 times a day, the average people do so only about 20 times. Smiling leads to a decrease in the stress-induced hormones that negatively affect your physical and mental health. *It has been observed that people who smile the most lived happier lives with happier marriages and fewer setbacks.*

It is the doorway for new friendships and a pleasant life. Remember what Victor Borges said: "Laughter is the shortest distance between two people." Smiles inadvertently signal that a person is less dominant, hostile or aggressive.

Everyone smiles in the same language. It is one of the things which make us different from animals. Dr. Kuhn has done a lot of study on smile and its positive effects. His newest book, "It all starts with a smile: Seven steps to being happier right now" helps you get more positive energy into and out of everyday life. *You can develop a better personality by learning to smile more meaningfully the whole day.*

The science of smiling. Experience a positive situation like seeing a friend you haven't met for a long time. Neuronal signals travel from the cortex of your brain to the brainstem and from there, the cranial muscle carries the signal further towards the smiling muscles in your face. Once the smiling muscles in your face contract, there is a positive feedback loop that goes back to the brain to reinforce your feelings of joy.

If you want to succeed in business, have more romance or friends in your life, smile more. When someone has a big smile, it shows they're willing to open up and expose a part of themselves. Over the long term, smiling can benefit your health, status at work place and social life.

- You can smile your way to a more agreeable, conscientious, and emotionally stable personality, according to a new research. Psychologists have found that none of the big grinners divorced later in life. In comparison, 25 per cent of the most straight-faced experienced divorce. A bigger smile may reflect a happy-go-lucky approach to life, the researchers reported. And bigger smiles may attract a happier partner, and lead to a happier relationship. A healthy smile can improve your overall health too.
- According to a study published in 2012 in the American journal **Proceedings of the National Academy of Sciences,** happy teens earned 10 per cent more income than average age at 29, while gloomy adolescents earned 30 per cent less than average at that age. That's why in a recent research scientists concluded that smiling can be as stimulating as receiving up a lot of cash.
- You can learn a lot from a smile. What you say with your smile speak volumes about you. When you put your best smile forward, you will make the best impression. The meaning of a smile changes depending on the social context. Some smiles bring benefits, but others reveal hidden weakness. Human smile vary depending on who they're talking to, the emotional set-up of the person, his attitude and the context. Smiles can reveal a lot.
- The subtle muscles of your mouth determine how you communicate at that moment. A dozen or so muscles connect with the circular muscles around your mouth and many more around your eyes combine to give different smiles.

Nice smiles are gentle and natural. Strike a smile you can hold for a long time. When you smile gently, your face looks relaxed. Your mouth opens slightly, and your lower lip matches the curve of your upper teeth.

Mona Lisa became one of the most famous paintings of all time because of her unique smile. Practising to smile like her will be a powerful tool for you. Upper and lower lips moving out half an inch and up to a 40-degree angle like she does is considered to be very beautiful.

A quick joyous smile flashes across your face when you see an old friend making your eyes squint and your neck muscles tense.

As you get older, you can work to change your smile as your teeth get worn as you age, let the soft tissue around your mouth descend to show your lower teeth instead of your upper. As teeth get shorter, this changes the tooth-to-gum ratio and gives a gummier smile.

Scientists have pin pointed more than 50 different types of smiles, and research suggests that the sincerest smile of all is **Smiling with your eyes—** a smile that pushes up into the eyes. When you engage your eyes— squinting them slightly to create small pillows under your eyes- instead of only your mouth, your smile has the power to charm other people. When you smile with your eyes, you're really feeling happy. Channeling good thoughts when you smile can help you appear to be more genuine. **It's very difficult to fake a smile when you smile with your eyes.**

Those who are truly skilled at smiling with their eyes can express happiness or mirth without moving their mouth. Only if you try to be positive and optimistic will real smiles appear on your face throughout the day.

Have confidence in your smile. If you are preoccupied with the colour and shape of your teeth, mouth odour and untidiness in dressing and grooming you will try to stifle your smile as you feel embarrassed. Look into whitening your teeth and getting rid of bad breath immediately. Otherwise, your smile will be fake and not genuine as you want it to be. Maintain your eyebrows and use a little eye makeup to make your eyes stand out beautifully.

Don't be self-conscious or think about yourself when you're talking to people. Look into the other person's eyes and see him or her. If you're genuinely glad to see the person, you'll break into a natural smile. When you're feeling nervous about how you are dressed up and groomed, how untidy you are-your smile will reflect them.

Try squinting. Lower your eyelids a bit and slightly squint and smile slightly with your mouth-without breaking into a full grin. It's more subtle than open smiling with your eyes, and it gives the impression that you're friendly and interesting. This may be more photogenic and romantic.

Laughing out loud at something funny is a great way to get you to smile. Laugh to your heart's content. But in the presence of strangers over-emotional outbursts may not be warranted.

Never give a fake smile (only moving the mouth muscles) to ridicule or belittle a person. Smile is meant as an expression of your happiness and to make another happy and it should not be to create tension and ill-feeling. Anyone can easily tell the difference between a real and fake smile.

There's no reason to frown. Even in the darkest of times there is something to look forward to. What is the good in getting upset or worrying over small things which are not the way you want them to be? There are ways to make you happy. Turn round your mind to something good that happened some time back. Listen to the lisping of your child or talk to a bosom friend or engage in something you love. Tomorrow it will all be better; the dark clouds will swim away and the brilliant sun will emerge from behind. Again there will be sunny days, warming rays and fragrant zephyrs. There is no meaning in a smile if one has not experienced a tear.

Stop beating yourself and stretch your facial muscles into a broad smile. Even if you smile when you are alone it has a positive impact to dissolve your tension or sadness. There are setbacks and failures and sorrow in everyone's life. Everyone worries too. If you are feeling bad about something past like say a terrible childhood, well, what can be done about it? Those who enjoyed a splendid one are lucky. But it is not their mistake you did not get a good one. They did not ask for theirs either. That is the way life is. Stop harping on your unpleasant past, brood and frown. There are many like the blind, the deaf, and the crippled, who are thousands of times more unfortunate than you. Many of them try to keep a smile and move. Then why not, you?

Chapter-27

The beauty in giving

Become richer by giving a portion of what you earn or what you possess. What goes out comes back. Selfless giving ensures manifold return. All the rich people of this planet are inclined to help others. And that could be one of the reason why they become richer. They get back what was given out in true charity, hundredfold. Giving is a sure way to receive more.

Blessed are those who can give without remembering. No wonder our present world is getting filled with those who want to give without any string attached. They are quick to part with a part of what they have earned as they know giving has a superior value when one does so quickly and not waiting for to be asked.

The best way you can evaluate a person is by how much he gives and by how much he feels for others in his wallet. Giving is always a thermometre of one's love towards others. When it comes to giving some people stop at nothing. 'Give all you can,' is an excellent formula for a successful life.

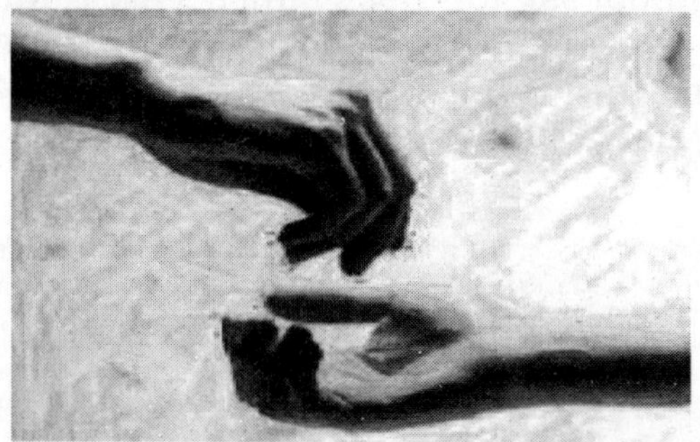

Warren Buffet has so far given in excess of $30.7 billion to healthcare, to alleviate extreme poverty, for education and for access to information technology. Bill Gates through Bill and Melinda Gates foundation has doled out close to 34 billion mainly to the development of education and AIDS prevention. Azim Premji from India has donated in excess of $2 billion for education and healthcare. Every rich man is known for a charitable frame of mind (that could be one of the reasons for their immense wealth)–what goes out comes back many fold.

All of us may not have the wealth, the time to do charity in a massive scale. Let us follow the advice of Mother Teresa: **"If you can't feed a hundred people, then feed just one."**

There is beauty in giving. The greatest souls that have grazed this planet are those who gave themselves up for others fully and unconditionally.

Let it be Mother Teresa, Gandhi, Father Damien, Martin Luther King Jr. or Abraham Lincoln, they surpassed all living souls with their selfless service to the needy.

As Winston Churchill once said, **"We make a living by what we get; we make a life by what we give."**

Our lives will be very much less fruitful if we are not giving what we have to others. It can be motivation, knowledge, riches, time, comforting words; it can be anything that alleviates others' pain or something that make others' life richer and more meaningful. It is this realization that motivates the rich philanthropists to give significant portions of their wealth to the poor.

Remember the ancient Chinese saying, 'a little fragrance always clings to the hand that gives roses.' There is another saying: 'The hand that gives is the hand that gathers.'

Those who have the attitude, 'May I serve you,' enjoy life far better than those who are constantly after material possessions, power or professional advancement.

Giving can be its own reward. But there is another aspect that a lot of us have failed to recognize. Giving is a form of energy that not only helps the recipient but it bounces back in a greater measure to the giver. The backward journey of this energy is often shrouded in mystery that the giver is not aware of it instantly nor is it immediately perceptible to the world at large. The giver receives more than what he gave out if he did so without any personal motivation whatsoever.

Even working more than you are paid for is a way of giving. By going the extra mile, you will not only become a valuable employee but you will also be rewarded hundredfold by the great Universal Watchdog who is a just employer. When you go out for an interview the added self-respect and esteem will make you ask for more pay as you know you are willing to give more than he is going to pay back to you.

The Bible mentions that whenever anyone feeds or clothes a destitute he does so to God himself. Well I think there is no good in the world which can come anywhere near the act of giving, selfless giving in particular.

- Even helping a blind person to cross the road;
- Feeding a beggar who is hungry;
- Giving little cash to someone who is in dire need and whom you do not know;
- Removing a stone from a foot path so that others are not hurt;
- Keeping a radiant smile as you crisscross the pathways of life;
- Sparing some time to take an injured stranger to a hospital;
- Giving out a certain portion of your wealth to the needy;

- Spending some time with the old to brighten their day;
- Offering your seat to an invalid in a crowded bus ....*are all acts of giving.*

Giving is the best way to receive. Everyone wants more and more. We are all brainwashed into believing we will be happy only if we have this and that and human wants are unlimited.

We have also heard the saying that 'true joy is in giving.' But very few of us experience it. Why? Because we don't give. Occasionally we do it for our own selfish motives. We give to charity so that others will think well about us or others will appreciate us. But giving without any strings attached-selflessly- is true joy. We understand the needs of others and try to fulfil them.

India has been a land famous for giving. In our religious scripts there are ample testimonies of big giving. Karna would give out anything asked for including his life-protecting shield. Giving is pure joy. Forget about the cost of what you give. Give whatever you can but anonymously. Give with the intention of benefitting the other person.

When you give, you will receive. Start giving today and shortly you will start receiving.

You can donate something to charity, give money to a beggar to have a square meal occasionally, say a good word when your colleague has done something good, take an injured on the road side to hospital or help a blind person cross the road. If you have nothing material to part with, give your love. A smile or a twinkle in your face when you meet others is a way of giving. You radiate happiness and joy. Hugging is a beautiful way of loving. We need hugs for well-being. Hug those you meet.

Pray for someone else. Every one of us normally prays for himself or herself. But switch your prayers for others. Wish them good and pray for good things to happen in their lives. This is a great way of giving. Whom should you pray for? There are millions around you who are poor, sick and suffering. Pray for them. When you pray you should feel it. Uttering words or passing thoughts through your mind detached won't help. Let a prayer be a good wish coming from the inner recesses of your mind. 'Praying for others' is definitely one of the noblest things you can do. It represents your desire to add value to others. Pray for the whole world, pray for your enemies. Any prayer is good for you and for those you pray for.

Living for others is the best way to live. That could be why Henry Drummond once said, 'There is true happiness only in giving.' Before we conclude let me remind you Arthur Schweitzer's words: "There is no higher religion than human service. To work for the common good is the greatest creed."

Chapter-28

Beat procrastination

Lazy people only think of doing things tomorrow or the day after. Problems and tasks are simpler or easier if you tackle them right now. Putting them off often ends up in you never doing it. Some of us wait and wait until the entire things have just disappeared. If you find somebody who brags about what he is going to do tomorrow, probably, he did the same thing yesterday too. He will only brag and never do anything substantial.

There is a saying, 'Tomorrow is the only day in the year that appeals to the lazy man.'

Why do you put off things?

It could be because the work is unpleasant or difficult or still you do not know how to do it. If the reason does not fall in one of these, you do so as you are lethargic or simply lazy. If the task is difficult, break it down into smaller elements so that each one does not look formidable. And then tackle them one by one until the whole lot is finished.

If you have too much to do, prioritize the whole thing. Do the most urgent ones first and so on; if there are tasks still to be completed assign them as the first priority of the next day. To avoid postponing you have to generate adequate interest to get the work done at any cost. If you have the habit of postponing, it will erode your self-esteem and confidence. Whatever is to be finished today has to be finished today itself. If you procrastinate for tomorrow, you will postpone it for the day after and then for the next day. The task will remain unfinished. If procrastination becomes a habit you are in a dangerous web of never accomplishing anything.

A common complaint for postponing is lack of time. This is only an excuse, a lame one at that. Because you have solid 24 hours each day like Mother Teresa, Leonardo Da Vinci, Abraham Lincoln, Michael Angelo or Gandhi. They accomplished so much and we are postponing our daily chores!

There is another beautiful principle. Time expands or contracts with work. If you have more work at hand, you finish each one faster. If there is very little to do you tend to take more time to finish a job requiring much less time. It is all in your hand. If you want to complete the entire work it can be finished on time.

If someone says, 'I do not have much time,' it only means he does not have much interest in that work. If one has genuine interest he will find time somehow. It is always lack of enthusiasm or direction and not lack of time.

Procrastination has a lot to do with time waste. If you do not know where and how your time goes waste, you may not be an efficient worker nor will you be able to do your tasks on time. You will procrastinate.

How do you waste your time?

It has been observed that 33% of all employed spend between 1-2 hours per day attending to their emails. 22% spend about 2 hours to do the same.

27% spend 1-2 hours per day surfing the net.

26% watch TV about 2 hours per day.

18% spend 1-2 hours for meetings.

16% spend 1-2 hours in non-business related conversations.

9 out of 10 spend 2 hours per day chatting.

About 90% of workers spend 1-2 hours travelling or commuting.

75% spend around 2 hours on twitter, Facebook, or such social media.

Almost all working people spend around 2 hours on cell phones.

Three fourths of workers think they waste their time due to stress or boredom.

The best way to combat time-killing is to make people aware of how they waste time and the value of the wasted time.

"Time is Money" —Benjamin Franklin The more time one wastes the more potential profit or career advancement you squander. And the best way to a better time-use is to track how you spend your time.

"Time is the secret resource and unless it is managed, nothing else can be managed."

—Peter Drucker

There is happy news: 1 out of 10 does not procrastinate; they are super productive. If you use all the time available to you efficiently the chances of procrastination fades away.

Sit up right now and decide to make up a list of things you plan to do. The list can be huge:

- Read the book you wanted to.
- Take your family for a movie or to dine out at a restaurant.
- Learn that thing a little more by surfing in the net.
- Make thorough enquiries regarding that product.
- Study about tax returns.
- Make the long pending phone calls.
- Finish the work before retiring today.

It is then that the movie you have been waiting for long, comes up in the TV. You watch it and sleep late. Naturally the work remains undone and you wake up late too. You procrastinate tasks until they grow too big and overwhelming. In the office, you end up doing just the absolutely urgent things and postpone the others. Just for today clear the backlogs of things you wanted to do for a long time. Reward yourself when you clear up the backlogs. An unfinished work is actually a burden on your mind.

If you have a great idea and you failed acting on it then and there, its appeal will die away with time and you will eventually forget it.

If you study the difference between the great people and the ordinary ones you will observe it lies in the way they spend their times. You need to be disciplined; you need to cultivate the 'do it now' habit. Treat time properly, if you idle it away you can never get it back. Organize it so that everything gets done before the deadline.

Chapter-29

Invest in yourself

"Generally speaking, investing in yourself is the best thing you can do. Anything that improves your own talents; nobody can tax it or take it away from you. ..If you've got talent yourself, and you've maximized your talent, you've got a tremendous asset that can return ten-fold."

—Warren Buffet

*I*f you strip the Ambanis of all their assets and dump them in the street… they would be back to a comfortable life with plenty of income in about a month. This would be the case too with Mittal, Bill Gates, Warren Buffet or Carlos Slim and the like. Why?

These people can walk into the headquarters of any major company on the planet, offer their services as a consultant and start earning a huge salary. They have built up such a rich human capital base. The stock of competencies, knowledge, social and personality attributes, including creativity, these people possess is huge. They have invested in themselves so richly that they are valuable anywhere any time.

What do you do to invest in yourself? We all invest money in the banks. But how many of us invest in ourselves? Is that not the greatest investment? Let us sharpen ourselves to gain an edge over others by acquiring more knowledge, skill and ability in our chosen field.

We all waste a lot of our time. If we make a simple time analysis of the way we spend each minute in our lives it would be easy to find that of the 24 hours available to us each day, we will be wasting about 3-4 hours or more. This includes time in front of the TV, sitting idle or day dreaming, chit-chatting with friends, boozing, going for movie, or loitering around the city centre. Even while we travel we can make use of the time by reading, recollecting, thinking about our goals or making new friends.

There is no greater crime than wasting our personal time. Investing in you will empower yourself. Investing in you is a must for anyone to achieve a better quality life now and in future, to be successful, productive, and satisfied. You have to invest for both personal and professional growth.

Improve your knowledge base, skills and abilities and polish your talents to grow personally and professionally.

Before we start dealing with the ways to invest in you, **establish what's most important for you in this life — what you will truly cherish and enjoy**. Visualize your ideal life –you need to grow stronger each day in mental, emotional and physical ways–regardless of how unattainable it may seem now –and act to manifest it one by one.

Decide to raise your self-worth. Even if you think you already possess enough self-esteem, work to improve your opinion of yourself. This calls for focused attention to improve yourself perhaps by utilizing more of your free-time.

Focus on your goals and life mission. The great secret to succeed is focus. If you dissipate your energy in this and that, you are not investing in yourself. Sharpen your mind and empower your body to achieve your chosen mission.

There are many avenues open to you to invest in yourself:

- Advance your education – take an extra degree/diploma/short-term course on line or otherwise in your chosen field.
- Learn a new language or improve language skills if you think it might help you.
- Enroll in workshops, attend conferences or participate in web-seminars in your line of work or business.
- Take pains to learn about every aspect of the operations of the firm you are working and master your work to become an invaluable asset to the company.
- Expand knowledge at a personal level: the entire knowledge is available on the net. You can also read books, articles, blog, anything related to the talent or skill you need in your career or business. Stay abreast of the latest trends or advancements in your field.
- Watch documentaries relating to your work or talent.
- Nourish and develop your creative side: write something, paint, sculpt, make pottery, make jewelry or design your own clothes.
- Find a like-minded group or community that's interested in your field of study, work or hobby.

- Brand your name on the net. Do you have an online presence? Why not create a visually appealing web page of yourself that provides your bio-data, contact information, accomplishments and skills. Next time you apply for a job or need to introduce yourself to someone online, just direct them to your resume page.
- Join a service club—you will meet a large number of people to enrich yourself.
- List five things that happened to you today, that you can be thankful about. This is to train your mind to look for the positive.
- Nurture your mind and broaden your vision: explore cultures by travelling, and meeting people from different backgrounds and listening to different styles of music. Engage in conversations with those who disagree with you and see their point of view.
- Care for your body and try to be healthy and fit as detailed in this book. If you don't practise the art of self-care, who will do it for you? Adopt healthy habits and take care of your body— the way you might maintain an expensive car. It will then perform marvelously for a very long time. Make healthy food choices, exercise daily, rest and relax. Get check-ups, take appropriate vitamins and become a positive person.
- You can practise yoga or meditation to reduce stress.

Investing in yourself will make a huge difference in your life, career, social life, well-being, and your ability to thrive and perform to the best of your ability. How much you invest in your mind and body will shape you, the way you interact with the outside world and improve the opinion you have of yourself. Your future is largely determined by your willingness and ability to invest in yourself now.

Let us equip ourselves so that we are more valuable at the market place and at home. We always decide our price. And today or tomorrow we will be paid what we are worth. It is up to us to increase our capital base.

"Investing in yourself is the best investment you will ever make. It will not only improve your life, it will improve the lives of all those around you."

—Robin S. Sharma

Chapter-30

Meditate each day

There is a lot of tension in today's life. On the road, at the workplace and at home life is full of stress. We are all on the run after money, possessions and to acquire more of everything. You may be caught up in the endless web of working and achieving more. There is no stopping any hour, any minute to relax or to feel at ease. Even our leisure gets crowded with movies, eating out and friends. There is no time for anything to ourselves and we become perennially tense. The speed with which our life is moving is alarming.

There is an information explosion. And we feel we are not able to catch up with the fast moving world! The faster you go the less control you have on it. The recklessness will tell upon your nerves, vital organs and they prepare for a strike. And to top it all you don't feel like living at ease; you don't enjoy the little good things of life and nature.

One of the best ways to slow down is to observe nature. Smelling a flower, observing a butterfly, hearing the murmur of leaves, being amidst verdant vegetation— all will invigorate you. Get away from this mad pace and be in nature. Feel a sunrise or sunset; observe how the clouds float on making designs or how the tree-tops sway in the wind. Take a long walk along the seashore watching the waves. You breathe in the beauty, the fragrance of the air, and the lullabies of Mother Nature. Observe the birds and plants around. Leave everything behind and spend time with nature and your inner self.

Every month take a holiday to nature locations. Hill stations are places to spend quality time. It will be an investment too. Be awake when the sun raises, birds chirping around and leaves rustling in the gentle breeze. The whole thing slows down your mind. In a fast paced life we require to slow down a bit. Let your body and mind cool down, your thoughts become clearer and calmer.

You will thus move much closer to your inner self becoming more intuitive and loving.

While indoors, you have to decide to shut off your mind and body to have a small rest, to get rejuvenated and to introspect. The best way to quite your body and mind is to be in solitude for whatever little time you can spare.

How to meditate?

Each day you spend a few minutes—thirty would be ideal—to quite your mind and its racing thoughts. Find a place—a closed room or an open place —where you will not be disturbed. (A sudden noise while meditating can be harmful). The sound of leaves rustling, birds twittering are good for meditation as you will feel one with nature. But you can also sit on a straight chair comfortably. As you practise mediation, you will be able to cut out external noises. When you meditate, the heart beat and breathing becomes slower.

Sitting cross-legged and straight with hands folded on the lap, on the ground, is considered to be the most ideal position.

Take four or five very deep slow breaths exhaling slowly after holding the air drawn in for a few seconds. It gives brain the essential oxygen to work clearly. Close your eyes and let your mind drift. Now start counting from ten to one slowly seeing each number in your mental eye. If you want deeper relaxation, count from 25 or even hundred to one. You concentrate on your breathing alone for a minute or so. Do not allow any thought to enter your mind as you do this. By now your nerves are rather quiet and your mind in solitude. Remember your mind would love to jump from thought to thought and from object to object. Holding it still will require practice and patience. But after practising this sort of mediation a number of times, the moment you start doing the breathing exercise your mind will get into a relaxation mode.

You can go to your favourite place—it can be a beach, a garden, a panoramic landscape, or any such scenic spot. Savour the sights, let each colour make ripples in your mind, feel and smell the air, feel the inner joy you felt whenever you went there. Hear each one of the sounds and go through the happy emotions you used to have. Continue this exercise for however long you can. Slowly open your eyes feeling happy and joyous. This simple exercise would refresh you. Do this for a few minutes each day.

When your thoughts become still, it lets you go deeper and you feel relaxed. Just like you can see the bottom of a still, tranquil lake you can reach to your innermost recesses of your mind. Meditation will make you more attentive and sharp. You will experience a feeling of well-being and calmness. Practise more silence and empower yourself.

Another way to mediate is to watch your thoughts without becoming a part of them. Like you see a movie projected on to the screen, your thoughts come and go without affecting you at all. Eventually you will notice you are becoming more and more peaceful.

Start concentrating on each thought that crosses your mind. Stop at every thought and study the thought. Soon you will notice it is easy to concentrate at these random thoughts. You will be slowly able to isolate each thought and remove it before you entertain the next thought. The final thing is to make your mind blank without any thought. You have now mastered your mind and become one with the universe. You are very close to 'Nirvana.'

Thought analyzing is another step of meditation. You may recall a particular thought and analyze it. This requires years of practise to be successful. Many great philosophers meditate on ideas like this and come up with new perspectives.

Use of mental sound is often good in meditation. The word Ohm is considered very good as it creates vibrations throughout the body. As you practise meditating with this mantra you will be tuned into meditative mode as soon as you start reciting ohm. Once you practise meditation you will notice marked improvement in your level of concentration. People who mediate regularly are able to face the problems of life more confidently and even their physical health improves. This tool is of immense help to keep your mind in control during a crisis.

You can alter the way you keep your mind quiet. Later you can opt to hold your mental screen without any thought for whatever time is possible. You can give self-suggestions to improve your personality. "Every day in every way I am becoming better and better" can be one of them. But merely repeating this won't do any good. Feel it as you say the words to yourself. You can use suggestions like 'I am confident', 'I am courageous', 'I am in perfect health both in body and mind.' 'I am becoming better and better'– Feel each aspect as you repeat the words. When you open your eyes experience a better, happier state of mind.

Meditation is an important tool for stress-free, successful, healthy and happy living. In India, it has been practised for ages by sages and rishis. The benefits of meditation have been well-documented over the years. Unfortunately not many people are unable to practise it mainly because they are not sufficiently motivated to do so. It is easy to meditate and still your mind for a few minutes each day as you have already seen. If you feel you need help, join a meditation group.

Improve your breathing technique

The basic concept is to improve your breathing, get rid of stale air from your lungs and make available plenty of oxygen in there. When you breathe shallowly only 30-40% of the air drawn in is taken out making stale, toxic air remain in your lungs. Breathing deeply in and exhaling deeply out will clear your lungs and make you relaxed.

Pranayam is a technique best suited for this. It teaches you how to inhale and exhale deeply using the stomach to push up and down on the diaphragm as required.

❖❖

Chapter-31

Become a good listener

Being a good listener can help you see the world through the eyes of others. It will enrich your understanding and expand your capacity for empathy. It also increases your contact with the outside world by helping you to improve your communication skills. Good listening skills can provide you with a deeper level of understanding about someone's situation, and help you to know what words are best to use and which words are best to avoid.

Listening is a consummate skill and there are many factors which will help you in this.

Let us first see the helpful body language factors.

- **Eye contact** is important when you are listening. If you give your friend the impression you aren't interested and are distracted, he may never open up to you. Focus your eyes, ears and your thoughts only on him/her and become a good listener. Try looking straight into their eyes to show you are listening, taking real interest in what they are saying.
- Look interested and meet the gaze of the speaker from time to time. But do not overwhelm the speaker by staring intently.
- **Remove all distractions** and give all your attention to the person who has something to say to you.
- **Adopt body postures**, positions and movements that are similar to the speaker. This will enable the speaker to relax and open up more.
- Turn your body towards the speaker. If you turn it away from the speaker, then it may look like you're itching to leave.
- Keep your hands and legs open and assume an open body language position. Do not cross your arms or legs.

- Watch the facial and body expressions of the "teller" to try to gather all information. Always be alert for things that have been left unsaid and for cues that can help you gauge the speaker's true feelings.
- Speak at approximately the same energy level as the other person.
- Be more observant of the speaker to have a better understanding of things.

Wait for the person to open: An active listener must be patient and let the speaker expose his or her full flow of thoughts, feelings and ideas. These may start as a trickle and may take a long time to develop fully. Too many probing questions will make the talker defensive and reluctant to share the information.

Assume you are in the other person's shoes. While listening, it is easy to get lost in yourself and consider the impact of the other person's words on you. Do not think about your response when you are listening. If you do so, your faculties just shut off. You must open out and look at the problems from the other person's perspective and assume that you are in their shoes.

Wait for the other person to ask your opinion before breaking the flow of their discourse with your probing questions or interruptions. Do not give direct advice unless you're asked for it. Instead, let the individual talk the situation out.

It is more beneficial to listen than it is to talk. When listening to people, engage fully in the conversation. *Remember that you have two ears and one mouth for a reason.* This means that you should be listening more than you are talking.

Instead of immediately judging the person who is speaking to you or come up with a solution right away, just take the time to listen and to look at the situation from the other person's perspective.

Avoid saying "I" or "me" a lot. This is a good indicator that you're focusing more on yourself than on the person's situation, problems or point of view.

If the person knows that you've had a similar experience, then he or she may actively ask for your opinion. In this case, you can offer it, but be cautious about acting like your experiences as they are exactly like the other person's. This might seem as though you are just trying to make fake situations to seem helpful. Remember no two experiences are even remotely similar.

- **Avoid comparing the person's experiences to your own.** Though you may think that the best thing you can do to really listen is to compare the person's experiences to your own, this is far from the truth. If the person is talking about dealing with a death in the family, you can share some wisdom, but avoid saying, “That's exactly like how it was with me.”

- Don't try to offer help immediately. Some people think that, when they're listening, they should find a quick and easy solution to the person's problem. This is not warranted. Instead, take what the person says at face value, and take the time to think of a solution when the person is speaking only if he or she is really looking for help in this way.
- Show them that you nod at appropriate times to show them you are listening. Also say little things such as 'Yeah' when the person is talking to you.
- If you want to be a good listener, don't interrupt in the middle of a point, Don't interrogate the person—you may gently put in your query when there is a pause. Never try to change the subject even if it is a little uncomfortable.
- Avoid giving advice like, everything will be alright, you will be much better in the morning and so on.
- Don't reply impulsively. Be silent and listen. Put aside your own anxieties or needs and wait patiently for the other person to unfold their thoughts at their own pace and in their own way.
- If the person is telling you something pretty private or important reassure him of your confidentiality—that whatever is said stays between you two. When you say it will be confidential keep it so unless the person is suicidal and requires help.
- Refrain from probing or putting the other person on the defensive. But use questions as a means by which the speaker can begin to reach his or her own conclusions about the issues being raised.

Some follow up is required for effective listening

Whatever the conclusion of the conversation, let the speaker know that you have been happy to listen and you are open to further discussion.

You can give a reassuring touch, even pat the speaker's hand or knee or put an arm around him or her. Do whatever is appropriate to the situation. You don't want to overstep your bounds when it comes to touching.

It's helpful to summarize and restate or repeat the main points to make the speaker feel you are listening. Offer to assist by giving any solution if you can arrive at one.

Remember what you've been told. If you don't remember names, details, or important events, then it would seem you weren't listening.

If you really care, then you should ask the person about the situation the next time you're together. Or you can call him/her or send a mail to see how the situation is progressing.

Chapter-32

Become humorous

"A sense of humour is part of the art of leadership, of getting along with people, of getting things done."

—Dwight D. Eisenhower

All of us know laughter is the best medicine. It is a stress-buster and tension-breaker. Humour and laughter has powerful medical benefits and they help build a pleasant state of mind and help sustain a positive personality. When it comes to relieving stress, more giggles and guffaws are what today's doctors tend to prescribe. A good sense of humour can't cure all ailments, but data mounting about the positive things laughter can do.

How does it improve your personality?

From a personality point of view:

- Humour is a key ingredient in creative thinking;
- It puts others at ease;
- It makes people less critical;
- It humanizes people;
- It can also help build trust;
- Numerous studies suggest that people who share a healthy, positive sense of humour tend to be more likable and are viewed as being more trustworthy;
- Humorous people are more approachable too;
- It helps you thus to get more friends.

Dozens of surveys suggest that humour can be at least one of the keys to success. A Robert Half International survey found that 91% of executives believe a sense of humour is important for career advancement; while 84% feel that people with a good sense of humour do a better job. Another study by *Bell Leadership Institute* found that the two most desirable traits in leaders were a strong work ethic and a good sense of humour.

Laughter is the key to success at work

It increases productivity too. But if your corporation is rigid and not open, there's a good chance your co-workers aren't cracking jokes or packaging information with wit and the chances to laugh at the workplace gets minimized.

Other benefits of laughter include:

- improvement of your immune system;
- relief from pain;
- coping up with difficult situations;
- improvement of your mood too.

It is also proven medically that anger, frustration and sorrow can bring in diseases including cancer. Widows, for instance, are much more prone to breast cancer than others. If you are depressed or sad your immunity gets reduced and the count of the white blood corpuscles comes down. A pleasant state of mind is conducive for health and well-being. **The facial features can change one's inner state of mind**. If your facial muscles can be turned into a laughing state, the intensity of sorrow will lessen and it will help maintain a pleasant state and build up the disease fighting mechanism.

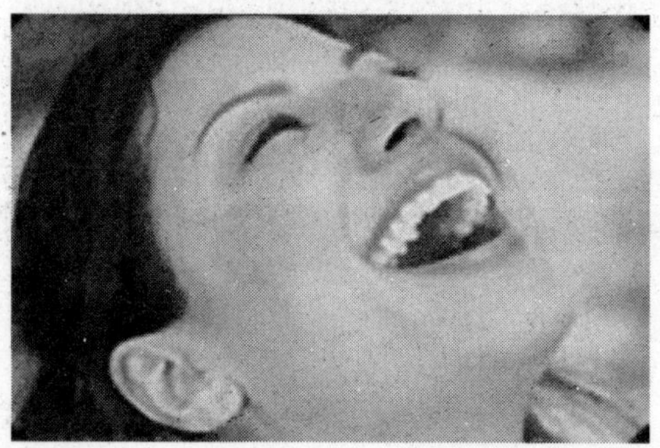

Constant laughing, smiles and a joyous state can cure diseases and help your body build up immunity against them. In a recent medical research, cancer patients were accommodated in a hall where they were allowed to read only funny magazines, articles, anecdotes and books, and see humorous films or videos. The experiment was continued for six months. When they were tested afterwards, it was observed that almost 20 per cent of the patients were cured totally! There was a marked improvement in the others!

Anxiety and tension can induce diabetes, asthma, bronchitis and even blood pressure. Depressing and negative thoughts force our glands secrete poison into the blood. It affects or retards the normal body functions like circulation, digestion and assimilation. Laughter induces a pleasant state of mind that helps bring out positive secretions facilitating all these functions.

How does a good laugh bring benefits?

Laughter enhances your intake of oxygen-rich air, stimulates your heart, lungs and muscles, and increases the endorphins that are released by your brain.

Laughter can also stimulate circulation and aid muscle relaxation.

Laughter can simply relieve your stress however intense it might be.

Many of you think you don't have a sense of humour at all. Well, it can be learnt as the ability is not inherited. How do you do that?

- See more funny movies.
- Read comic magazines and humorous cartoons that make you chuckle.
- Spend more time with friends who can make you laugh.
- Practise laughing, even forced ones are OK. Try simply to laugh more each day.
- Don't laugh to hurt another or ridicule a colleague. Use it to share warmth and happiness.
- Join a laughter club and simply laugh with them.
- Make work places more relaxed and open to generate laugh.
- Use humour with your colleague.
- Encourage family members to be more humorous in these ways.

Everybody loves a person who can make them laugh and bring a lighter touch or perspective to everything in life. One does not need to be all serious and sober all the time. Becoming humorous or funny every once in a while will turn you into a more charming personality.

But all cannot be equally humorous but trying to be funny is worth it. Feeling tired? Try laughing more. Some researchers think laughter just might be the best medicine to get revived, helping you feel better and putting that spring back into your step.

Now try laughing. Even if it has to be forced it's OK. Once you've had some hearty laugh see how you feel. Your mind and muscles would have become more relaxed.

"I believe that if people can get more laughter in their lives, they are a lot better off."

—Wilson (psychologist and laugh therapist)

Chapter-33

Enjoy what you do

"Don't aim for success if you want it; just do what you love and believe in, and it will come naturally."

—David Frost

One of the timeless secrets of a long and happy life: pursue a work that you can enjoy. The common denominator of the happiest souls is that they all loved their work. It was fun for them. They did not work a single day. It was all play and work. The truly successful ones simply pursued their goals without knowing whether they were working or playing.

This is the greatest criteria you should bear in mind in selecting a job. Not the pay and perks. Not the management and the working climate. Not the scope for promotions. Not the pension or the distance from your home or anything else. It need not be a regular job; you follow what your mind is after. It can be photography, singing, painting, bird-watching, animal or plant love, nature conservation, fashion, movie direction, sculpture, selfless service, whatever. The question is: **'Will you enjoy doing it?'** Will you be able to develop a passion for it? Choose a profession which you will enjoy, which will be like a hobby to you.

When you love what you do, money will start coming. Don't worry about it at all. If, on the other hand, you went into a profession to please others or got attracted by the pay, perks and other benefits, you will regret it the whole of your life. That will be the greatest sorrow of your life.

A career is not a destination, it is the journey. So what kind of a journey you must choose? It should be a journey which you can enjoy. You can excel with consistency only at tasks that you love doing. Enjoyment does not mean that the task is easy, or that you know how to do it, all that it means is you, love doing it.

Generally we do not think what kind of work we should choose and simply accept a job offered to us. The package may be good, the company may be excellent but we do not take time to reflect whether we will enjoy the work. No wonder there are thousands who regret that their work is boring. Already a few years have slipped by. Now to change this job and locate another one looks to be daunting and they go on grinding at the work grudgingly. And life seems to be a total failure for these guys.

How to pick up a career you will like?

We are all poor at it. We think we are picking a good job and then it turns out to be a bad job. It may be quite difficult to pick a good job unless you take time, know the job well and check whether it will suite you temperamentally and so on. We simply accept what comes our way.

Economist Neil Howe says that only 5% of people pick the right job the first time. He calls those people "fast starters" and in general, they are less creative, less adventurous, and less innovative, which makes a conventional, common job OK for them. So it's questionable whether you should even aspire to be one of those people who picks right the first time. But you cannot go on hoping from one job to another until you find something you like. No one wants to hire a 40 year old who hasn't stayed in the same job for more than a few years. Well, at the start of your career you can jump and try a few jobs but you should be able to land at the right one in a few years.

How do you find out what you love?

- Know your innate talents, likes and dislikes.
- Know what you enjoyed doing best in your free times.
- What type of work has got you absorbed fully in the past?
- Are you an introvert or extrovert? Introverts can't like a sales, teaching or public relations job, not anything to do with meeting people.
- Are you good in details or are you satisfied with an overall picture? If you love detail, may be accounting, research, labs will be suitable for you.
- If you are artistically bent, find a job suiting your talent. Or simply follow your line of interest. It can be painting, singing, drawing, writing– anything that suites you intrinsically.
- Are you a self-starter with leadership abilities or a follower who would like to obey all rules and do what is told--Choose your job accordingly?
- Do you like meeting people and convincing them? Go for sales or business development.
- Do you have financial intelligence? If yes, go and start a business.

- Are you spiritually inclined? If yes, select a spiritual line— become a priest or nun.
- Do you have a flavour for writing? If yes, choose a writing career.

In India, they have a UGC test as a basic criteria to become a teacher. This examination is purely objective and in no way connected with the aptitude of the person. No wonder many of our university teachers are total failures in their profession. Somehow they spend the time in the class and earn the huge money paid by the government.

A job is a bread winner for the majority. They work to live and never bother to contribute something, go the extra mile or do more than they are expected of. They don't love what they do and they do the bare minimum and keep the job. They lose the charm of life without any fulfilment—and live a vegetable existence.

Career planning

Choosing a career can be confusing, complicated and sometimes depressing. With so much pressure from your family and the urge to follow your dreams and to become a success in life, you need to plan your career and spend time to see the one most suited for you. The first and foremost question you will ask yourself is, 'Will it let me follow the passion of my life?' You cannot choose something for someone else. Can I be successful in this job? Will I make as much money as I want?

While we are heading into the unknown, desire is all-important. You simply want to be doing something that you love, or something that is logically going to lead you to something you love, in order to do your best. That desire will make you more creative and more resourceful, and will help you get further faster. It will help you persist. When you're trying something that's never been attempted before — beginning an unusual project, or trying to get a new business off the ground — you're going to face a lot of obstacles. You don't want to be giving up the first time you encounter one.

Well it may not be all that easy for all to find out one's true passion. Those who do are lucky and they succeed in life very fast. The successful people usually find out their passion and start working for it quite early in life.

Chapter-34

"Your work is to discover your world and then with all your heart give yourself to it."

—Buddha

Mobile skills

Mobile phones have become an integral part of modern life. The advances in mobile technology have far reaching influence in all aspects of man's life. Social interaction has been almost revolutionized by the mobile phones. Contemporary mobile-phones have not only speaking and messaging facilities but they have a camera, GPS and they can be used to access the internet, and audio-video content.

We now rely on the smart phones for everything. It helps us coordinate our lives; it provides us with a sense of safety and gives us accessibility to anything and everything. You can call someone in the farthest continent, send a mail to anyone anywhere, chat with your friend on facebook or twitter, access any knowledge from the net, hear your favourite songs, watch a movie and complete the notes you have been working on. Your Mobile is your true friend, helper and supporter.

It is imperative that all of us must be conversant with its use and be familiar with all the applications possible with today's high tech pieces. If you are not mobile savvy and mobile friendly you will be missing a lot of easiness in living in the modern world.

Smartphones are often the fastest way to get things done at the workplace these days. Text whenever something is urgent or important. You can even communicate outside office hours. Both of these enable you to work in the moment.

As the mobile phone supports interpersonal interaction, its use might be a function of your personality. **Sociolinguistic studies show that males and females often communicate differently with mobiles.** The gender literature suggests females are more linguistically polite than males. Gender is just one variable that comes into play in how we use mobile phones. In a number of instances, culture may be the critical issue. Americans have been seen avoiding strangers by pretending to talk on their phones. Italians do not use their phones while sitting at dinner with their families. Koreans are heavy mobile phone users. There are so many such national traits.

Extroverts reported spending more time calling, and changing ring tones implying the use of the mobile phone as a means of stimulation. Introverts and perhaps disagreeable individuals were less likely to value incoming calls.

Mobile phone use is banned or regulated in some circumstances or areas. Some people do not refrain from using mobile phones even there. Such problematic mobile phone use can be considered to be an addiction-like behaviour. Phone-related driving hazards are many and generally drivers are advised not to use mobiles while on the wheel.

It is good mobile practice to:

- Attend to the incoming call immediately. It is incorrect to let it ring for long.
- Check your messages at least once a day. There can be a lot of junk mail but urgent messages need your attention and reply.
- Follow good telephone manners while calling or answering a call.

Many of us often use our phones on the bus, in parks, cafés, on bikes, in the streets, in shops— sometimes shouting or yelling, sometimes becoming intimate. Today, with all our mobile devices, we can be rude anywhere at any time. Such random, uncaring public use of the mobile phone has necessitated certain mobile phone manners.

The ways mobile phones can cause offense to others are aplenty. Hence you better heed some of the rules while using them.

- Your mobile phone conversation should not disturb others. Intimate and angry exchanges are never permitted in public.
- Put your cell phone on mute or turn it off during meetings and public performances.
- Commit not to talk on your cell phone in elevators, libraries, museums, restaurants, theatres, places of worship, funerals, and other public places.

- Keep your cell phone conversations private, rather than subjecting others to your conversations.
- Keep calm and avoid displaying anger and becoming emotional during a call in a public place.
- People who talk on the phone or send out text messages while they check out at the grocery store or pay at a drive-through, make the cashier wait, and hold up the line. This is incorrect.
- Walking while texting or emailing is annoying to watch. Teenagers are notorious for doing this. Some crazy young men ride a bike while texting.
- Sitting on a public or private toilet while talking to someone on your phone is disgusting. Wait until you finish your business. What if the person, you're conversing with, figures out what you are doing?
- Snapping unsuspecting people or sharing photos and videos are not good. That's why, for obvious reasons, in many places they ban use of cell phones.
- Avoid calling or texting when you are with people engaged in a conversation. If a call is important, apologize and ask permission before accepting it. Respect those who are with you and give them your complete and undivided attention. When you're in the company of others, let voice mail handle non-urgent calls.
- Be mindful of your volume. People normally talk three times louder on a cell phone than they do in a face-to-face conversation. This is not a good practise.
- Don't put your mobile phone on the table while seated for lunch or dinner. Never call or talk to another while you are eating.
- Don't make restaurant staff wait to serve you as you are on a mobile. If you are in queue do not make others wait for you. If the call is important, get out of line.
- Don't use mobile while driving. Your life and that of others are more important.
- Don't argue over the mobile when others are present. One-sided screaming is irritating.
- Don't use unparliamentary words in public or in private.
- Respect the personal space of others. When you must use your phone in public, keep say, a 3m. distance between you and others.

- If you lose reception, live with it. Refrain from shouting into a dead device. Ring the other person as soon as it is regained even if it is to say goodbye.
- On public transport avoid talking loud so as not to disturb your fellow passenger. Use them in trains and buses only if they won't disturb others.
- Do not use mobiles in hospitals and other health-care institutions, where life-support equipment is installed and operated.
- Use of the mobile phones are prohibited on board aircrafts.

Good cell-phone etiquette is similar to common courtesy. All cell-phone users should be thoughtful, courteous and respect the people around them.

Chapter-35

Control your emotions

Psychologists agree that IQ contributes only about 20% of the factors that make up one's success. A major chunk of the other factors emanate from what is known as emotional quotient. Knowing one's emotional level, ability to control it, understanding others' emotions and responding to them accordingly are essential for success in family, profession and social lives.

Team-work and interpersonal skills

You could have been the top grader in the university and an outstanding performer but if you fail in being a successful team player you will be pushed out. If you develop conflicts and friction with others you will be graded lower and later removed altogether from the corporation. Success of any organization today depends on the co-operation of people and one must have good emotional, interpersonal and communicative skills. Every management wants to build congenial relationships even in the most difficult and critical situations. You must have empathy to understand every other member and build trust with each one of them that will bind you with others like a successful soccer team. One has to adjust to opposing views, or be able to live with people of diverse backgrounds, and personality traits. You have to be agreeable, concerned of others, and helpful and must be willing to conform to the team rules and ethics. Success is not yours alone, it belongs to the team and you must be happy as a part of it.

Being an effective group member is a critical factor in today's world. To function successfully even in a small group, one must be capable of communicating clearly, intellectually and emotionally.

- You should be able to explain your own ideas and feelings in an open but non-threatening way.
- Listen carefully to others.
- Ask questions to clarify others' ideas and emotions.
- Try to understand how others feel based on their body language.
- Try to resolve conflicts, differences of opinion and tensions.

Regular and open communication is a must among group members; they should share their thoughts, ideas and feelings; they should trust and support each other.

Employment authorities consistently mention collabouration and teamwork as being a critical skill, essential in almost all working environments. One needs to develop self-awareness, self-control, understanding others' emotional level and responding accordingly, social awareness, and empathy to become a good team player. The whole spectrum of these can be termed emotional intelligence.

Here are some questions which might acquaint you with regard to your emotional status.

1. Are you aware of your feelings of insecurity, inferiority, irritability and anger? Yes/No
2. Do you think you have very little control over your mood—even very small occurrences can make you happy or very sad? Yes/No
3. Does the brighter side of things appeal to you generally and you feel optimistic most of the time? Yes/No
4. Do you become sad or desperate often? Yes/No
5. Do you tell yourself, 'this is my fate'; 'I'm not going to succeed however I try?' Yes/No
6. Do you have clear goals and an 'I can' attitude? Yes/No
7. Are you able to control your emotions and respond to problems calmly? Yes/No
8. Are you able to understand others' emotions and empathize with them? Yes/No
9. Are you able to cope up with stress and tension patiently? Yes/No
10. Do you accept yourself as you are with all your strengths and weakness? Yes/No

Correct Answers: Yes: 1, 3, 6, 7, 8, 9, 10. All others must be 'No'. Give 1 mark for each correct answer.

Score 9-10 good emotional control; 5-6 sometimes you have control; and sometimes no. 1-4 emotionally unstable.

Your aim should be to belong to the first group. All leaders and people with good personality are always in that category. It is estimated that,

20-30% of all adult population goes through severe emotional problems. They become sad; suffer from insomnia, fatigue and even suicidal thoughts.

Can you blow away your blues of life? Doing regular exercise, having more friends and an all-consuming goal, volunteer work/community service, going out with a friend or family more, smiling and laughing often and doing regular meditation can help you overcome your blues.

Happiness and sadness are the most basic emotions according to neuro-psychiatrics. We have dealt with these emotions quite in detail with steps to become happy and contented. According to Lincoln, "Most folks are as happy as they make up their minds to be. Our happiness depends on how we perceive and view our circumstances rather than what they really are. Enjoying what one has at the moment is the best thing to be happy." **Icelanders** despite living in a wind-swept island surrounded by glaciers and volcanoes are found to be the happiest people in the world.

Is anger your worst enemy? If you are prone to becoming angry often there cannot be a worse enemy in your life. It is not easy to overcome this tendency too. The following simple tips might help you.

- Beware that you are prone to become angry at the slightest provocation. This awareness is the first requirement to control it.
- Do daily meditation for 20-30 minutes.
- Engage in physical exercise for at least half an hour each day.
- If you are always busy with work, take time out, go for picnics, tours and trips to scenic locations.
- If you can hold your response for a while when anger tries to burst out you may be able to control it.
- Make wins every day and become an achiever in life.
- Try to be more humorous as detailed in the concerned chapter.

Are you the anxious kind?

Feelings of anxiety, dread, fear and tension overpower us all at one time or another. If they become persistent and intense over long periods of time they can produce life-long harmful effects. You need to see that they are under control. How do you know whether you are a victim of these?

1. Does criticism greatly affect you?
2. Do you worry a lot?
3. Do you get upset by even a small noise?
4. Do you fear you may lose your dear one?
5. Do you often worry about your health?
6. Are you uneasy to meet one from the opposite sex?

7. Do you feel uneasy to wait for something?
8. Do you feel you have not locked the door after coming out?
9. Are you afraid of death?
10. Do you feel lonely often?

If your answer is yes to most of them you are an affected person. How do you know if you are in a state of panic? If your heart is racing or pounding, if your face is flushing or if you are shouting and saying unreasonable things, you are in panic.

How to control anxiety?

- Take some deep slow breaths and count from 10 to 0 slowly.
- Find out exactly what you are afraid of? Check the facts.
- Write down your present anxieties.
- Take a decision to overcome the fear or anxiety.
- Remember 90% of all the worries never happen.
- Regardless of a bad occurrence things will change for the better. They always do.

Learn to be assertive by learning the art of saying 'no' when required

There is no need to please everyone by acceding to their request. If you feel you can't give what he asks be firm and say no. Requests for your time are coming in from all quarters through phone, email, or in person. To stay productive, to be assertive and minimize stress, you have to learn to say no.

- It's important to be polite, but being nice by saying yes all the time will only hurt you.
- Instead of saying 'no' bluntly you can tell him you require time to think it over.
- Tell the person you will give a thought and get back to him later.
- Say 'no' to your boss if required. Taking on too many commitments may weaken your productivity.
- Forewarn your colleagues and bosses before the meeting starts that you are already full and you cannot take any new assignment.
- If you think the request made isn't good, tell that it does not suite you.
- *Don't buy something you do not really need*— this is a way of learning to say 'no'.

Our Self-image: It is the way you see yourself. It is the self you think you are. It is highly private and each one of you alone is an expert in your self-image. It has been influenced by the way we have been treated by our parents, relatives, school mates and others. Overly critical parents make their child of low self-opinion.

Our ideal 'self' on the other hand, is the 'self' we would like to be, including our ideals, aspirations and values. Our ideal 'self' must be an incentive to do our best. Your aim should be to become a likeable, attractive, successful, assertive, confident and honest person able to control your emotions. A high level of self-acceptance, well-adjustment and adaptability help one to live more spontaneously and with acceptance from others.

Chapter-36

Computer skills

"I think it's fair to say that personal computers have become the most empowering tool we've ever created. They're tools of communication, they're tools of creativity, and they can be shaped by their user."

—Bill Gates

Computers have considerably changed the lives of human beings and today the majority of us cannot imagine our lives without them. Computers make people's lives easier and more comfortable: they provide opportunities for staying in touch to billions of people who may very well be in different parts of the world. The technology has advanced so much that today people can drive computerized cars, doctors can diagnose dangerous diseases, manufacturers can produce perfect goods in the factory and many can work for employers from other countries without even seeing them. Several programmes can be simultaneously run in modern day computers and execute instructions of a magnitude faster than human perception. The computer has significantly changed our world through advances in science, medicine, business, education, effective communication and negotiating.

Be proficient in computer and get far

Computer is an electronic brain that people can rely on and is crucial element to business people, professionals, students, and home makers. Because of the continually increasing use of computers in our daily communication and work, the knowledge of computer systems and the ability to work with it with relative ease is essential requirements for many positions. The degree of knowledge and proficiency required varies from one position to another based on the tasks and duties involved.

You can't get far in today's world without being able to use a computer proficiently. Successful people have systems in place to help them find what they need and when they need it. Computers help them quickly locate the information required to support their activities.

Computers help in decision-making

We are living in the information age where, on a daily basis, we are constantly exposed to an ever growing and rapidly changing pool of information. Computer gives access to them and they keep us abreast of the various developments. One needs to respond quickly and effectively with the latest information for accomplishing anything. Decision making is possible only with the all required information. Google is a gateway to nearly infinite knowledge; it has indexed websites containing information on just about everything and everyone. One needs to have computer proficiency to access them.

One needs to be good at using a computer and should be able to use Microsoft Word, Excel, PowerPoint, Access or other standard business-required programmes with relative ease.

Health issues

Technology has truly become an inseparable part of our lives and an essential tool in every field. But, with increasing number of computer users, the number of health issues is also growing at a rapid pace. If you work in front of a computer for a few hours that too once in a while you may not be at a health risk. But if you spend about 4 hours or more everyday then you should probably keep a check on these health issues. Those who spend a lot of time in front of the screens of their computers suffer from the lack of physical activity. They often suffer from muscle soreness and fatigue. They also get back-pain, chest pain, numbness in arms, shoulder and feet. If your posture is not correct, these types of problems will be accentuated. Either you are sitting on an uncomfortable chair or you are not able to maintain correct posture.

- Your screen should ideally be at your eye level or lower.
- Sit with your back straight and legs perpendicular to the floor with feet resting flat on the floor.
- Elbows can rest at the sides.
- Don't sit continuously for long periods. Stretch a bit at intervals.
- Take mini-breaks and go for a short walk.
- Type softly. Adjust your mouse by the side of the keyboard.
- Move the mouse with your entire arm and not with wrist alone.
- Sit at the correct distance from the screen. Look elsewhere and blink occasionally.

- Keep your neck straight when in front of the computer and circle your neck at times to release the strain.
- Let your wrists not rest while you are typing; but hold them up in line with the backs of your hands.
- Hold the mouse lightly, don't grip hard or squeeze it.

One of the chief medical problems associated with computer-related work is **carpal tunnel syndrome (CTS)**— a stress-related injury caused by repetitive movement of joints, especially the wrist, and can lead to numerous musculoskeletal problems. This problem is caused by the wrist-alone usage of the mouse, keeping the wrists at rest while typing and by crouching towards the screen while typing.

In many cases, frequent computer users suffer from **computer vision syndrome**, which can result in severely reduced eyesight (Myopia), blurred vision, overall eye tiredness and even Glaucoma.

Prolonged computer use and sedentary lifestyle can make you stressful and contribute to obesity. All these can be avoided by taking appropriate steps and following the latest tips (given above) to overcome them.

Your computer can know your personality better than your friends

Whenever you use a computer, you leave behind a lot of personal information and computers can use that to understand your personality. Researchers from Stanford University in California and the University of Cambridge have performed a study which compared the personality traits of 86,000 participants acquired via a questionnaire with an analysis of their Facebook activity.

Where the team had gathered data from over 100 Facebook likes (articles, videos, artists and other items)for a person, their algorithms could determine a person's personality more accurately than their friends and family. The analysis need not be confined to Facebook alone; there are so much evidence left behind by you in your computer—the websites you visit, the mails you sent and receive, the purchases you make, your activity in social media, what you write or what pictures you store-could all be used to determine what kind of a person you are.

A computer's reach of you is very limited as of now. It can only know a few of your traits. Psychologists normally analyze hundreds of your dimensions to build an accurate picture of you and your behaviour. But there are researchers who feel artificial intelligence will be able to draw inferences about a person as accurately as a spouse in the near future.

There are some computer ethics all of us must follow:

1 Always use computers in such a way that it insures consideration and respect for your fellow humans.

2. Do not use or appropriate other people's intellectual output without permission or payment.
3. Do not steal CDs, pen-drives, or mouse balls.
4. Let nothing of what you do in computers harm or hurt others. You cannot spread rumours or false propaganda or circulate photos that will pain others.
5. Do not peer into other people's files or data without their permission.
6. Do not use pirated software or CDs that do not have a copyright (for which you have not paid).
7. Use computers to build positivity, self-image and confidence. Spending time with undesirable sites may cause harm to your personality.
8. Do not get addicted with computers.

In the current world, it's almost impossible to imagine that someone can live without a computer. It is one of the most brilliant gifts of science constantly being updated to make our lives better. We have all come to rely on this wonderful electronic brain in our everyday life. It has proved a friend and servant of us everywhere. Having adequate knowledge to use it efficiently is just a basic requirement of modern life. We should also take care to see that we are careful not to harm others in any way and protect ourselves from wrong practises and usages.

"The internet could be a very positive step towards education, organization and participation in a meaningful society."

—Noam Chomsky

Chapter-37

Grooming and hygiene

Grooming and hygiene are fundamental to a good personality. One has to pay close attention to these in order be a confident person and succeed in the modern world.

Personal hygiene implies we should be clean at all times. Soap and water are essential for keeping the skin clean. Bathe or shower yourself twice (at least once) each day—including holidays. Clean every cell of your body. A mild soap will do the job adequately. Germicidal or antiseptic soaps are not essential for the daily bath. You can use a bath sponge for scrubbing. Back brushes and heel scrubbers are available. But do not use abrasive material.

Many do not take care to clean the webs of toes, underknees, between legs, inside ears, underarms, backside and so on. The genitals and the anus need to be cleaned well because of the natural secretions of these areas. Unhygienic conditions here can cause irritation and infection. We normally do a quick job and rub ourselves to put on our clothes and move out. Bathing is to be a carefully carried out activity, taking time to make sure our body is totally and fully clean. Wash off well after soaping. Drying with a clean towel is important. Avoid as far as possible sharing soaps and towels. This is all the more important as we live in a hot country with a lot of dust. Those who are involved in active sports or work out to a sweat should take a bath after the activity each time. Change into clean underwear after bath.

Around middle age, the skin tends to go dry a bit. A moisturizing oil or cream can be used. It is better to use this at night, because if you go out in the sun or commute on dusty roads when the skin is hot and humidity high, dust will stick to it.

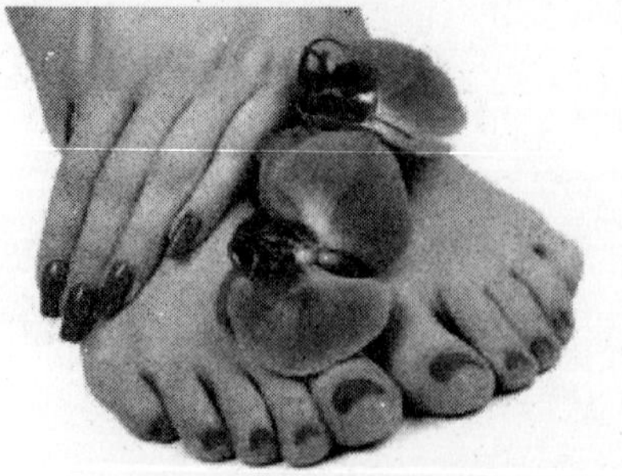

Nails

A healthy body ensures healthy nails. Brittle or discoloured nails show up deficiencies or disease conditions. Cut the nails of your fingers and toes at least once a week.

Grow nails only if you can keep them clean. Short nails make less trouble. Clip nails short, along their shape. Don't cut them so close that it pinches the skin. Do not keep your nails painted continuously. It causes the keratin, of which nails are made, to split. Go for a **manicure** for your hands and nails once in a month or so. They will soak your hands in warm water for ten minutes, massage your hands, and do a thorough cleaning and shaping of the nails.

Give your feet a thorough scrub with a sponge, or foot scrubber that is not made of very abrasive materials. **Pedicure-** a similar process like manicure for feet-once in a month - is good to keep your toes and feet neat and tidy.

Teeth

Brush teeth twice a day and rinse well after every meal. Brushing before going to bed is important. While brushing, pay attention to the fact that you are getting rid of the food particles stuck in between the teeth and in the crevices of the flatter teeth at the back, the molars and pre molars. Brush down on the upper teeth and brush up on the lower teeth. Pay attention to the tongue and the inner surface of teeth as well. The brush should have resilient bristles. It should be rinsed well and left to dry after use. There are no perfect toothpastes or powders. Use one without harsh abrasives or strong antiseptics.

Avoid bad odour: Some of you are naturally more prone for bad odour than others. Getting rid of smoking, drinking more water, consuming juices of raw vegetables, and oral hygiene will help you. Fenugreek tea has been found to cure bad breath too.

If you have **bad body odour** that is to be taken care of immediately. It travels ahead of you. The most odour emanating areas are armpits, feet and genitals as they are fully covered throughout the day. Fungi can also cause it.

- The best remedy is always proper body hygiene and cleanliness.
- Overuse of powder may not help; they clog up the sweat glands.
- Using anti-bacterial deodorant soaps will help.
- Having a shower or two will wash away the bacteria that produce bad odour.
- Avoid using meat, too much alcohol, garlic and caffeine.
- Include more fresh fruits, vegetables, whole grains into your diet.
- Drink a lot of water.
- Repeatedly wearing unwashed clothes or socks can cause severe odours.

Dressing

The first impression an individual wafts around depends on the way he/she is dressed and groomed. We cannot change our physical features or colour but we can change our appearance by dressing smartly and being hygienic always. It does not mean you need to go after the latest fashion that looks fantastic with the model or celebrity.

- Choose clothes/dress that fits you or that which you like and suited for the occasion.
- Wear fresh, neat and well pressed clothes each day.
- You have to be professionally dressed in the office. You cannot go in shorts and T-shirt —casuals or use deep-red or yellow- coloured outfits. You may choose subdued shades of grey, blue or white. This may not apply always to ladies.
- You need not spend a fortune on your clothes, but go for good choice— what suites your body and your colour, keeping with the improvements in tailoring.
- Avoid the habit of putting the same dress we wore yesterday-soiled or unsoiled. This will increase your body odour and make you feel less confident than when you have fresh clothes.
- Even socks have to be changed every day.
- You can use mild but elegant perfumes on your dress –if you like it —to add up to your confidence levels.

Footwear

We do not pay much attention to our footwear unlike the developed world. Many are still going to the office in 'chappals' and those who use shoes are not careful to keep them polished and shining. Footwear is an integral part of your personal attire and all care has to be taken to see that it is also neat, polished and elegant. Again branded ones will add to your appearance.

- Those who use shoes constantly need to slip them off now and then. This airs the socks a bit and makes them less smelly.
- Wear cotton socks.
- Wear a clean pair every day.
- Powder your feet before wearing socks. Many people have sweaty feet, and socks and shoes can get quite smelly.
- If possible do not wear the same pair of shoes every day. Keep at least one more pair and use it alternatively.
- Go for a pedicure once in three weeks.

These are small things but they inevitably add to the way you feel about yourself.

Hair

It is your crowning glory. A good head of hair can add much to your appearance and sex appeal. If you are blessed with hair, take enough care to maintain it in style. Ladies can wash their hair at least once a week using soap or mild shampoo. Rinse well. Dry your hair after a wash. Brush your hair three to four times a day with a soft bristled brush or a wide toothed comb. Wash your brush and comb every time you use it. Oil the scalp, once a week, preferably an hour before hair wash.

Men should take care to adopt a professionally good hairstyle. It may not be advisable to go after the hair fads of soccer or cricket players or even singers. Keep your beard and mustache trimmed, cleaned, and styled properly. If you don't, it can seriously affect your looks. You may shave off facial hair but if you keep them make sure they are organized and tidy. Get a beard trimmer and use it at least once a week. You have to find the right style for your beard and mustache. Clean both of them every day.

Hands

The world around us is full of micro-organisms. Some bacteria are found on our bodies too. As we eat and prepare food with bare hands extra attention has to be paid to the cleanliness of hands. Sticking dust and grime is not good anyway. Wash hands thoroughly with soap and water before and after every meal and after visiting the toilet. Soaping and rinsing should cover the areas between fingers, nails and back of the hand. Hands should be dried with a clean towel after wash. The towels have to be washed and changed each day.

Menstrual hygiene

No woman feels completely comfortable when she has her period. Technology offers a variety of stuff to deal with the flow. You have to decide what suits you best. Sanitary pads can become noticeable in tight fitting clothes. They can cause some soreness on the inner thighs too. Some women use tampons instead of external pads. The plug of absorbent cotton or gauze inserted inside should not be left unchanged beyond six hours. They may cause 'toxic shock.' The menstrual cup put in collects the flow and can be emptied, cleaned and reused. Washing is important. Bathing is essential to get a feeling of freshness. Some women suffer from the problem of odour during menstruation. Cleanliness and change of sanitary pad/tampon often will reduce this problem. Using powder or perfume is generally not recommended by experts.

Chapter-38

Develop your character

Character describes who you are. It is the sum of your qualities. It can be of moral or ethical strength, and it contains your attributes, traits and abilities. It defines you and this is what guides your actions.

Character is your signature and it is unique. No one else will have your character. Every society places a lot of importance on it. In Japan, for instance, big corporate honchos commit suicide if there is a blemish on their character.

It has been formed based on your inheritance, childhood experiences, thoughts, beliefs and the inner moral light you follow.

The greatest attribute of character is perhaps **integrity** which is in essence the steadfast adherence to a strict moral or ethical code. There isn't any personality attribute that is more important than one's ethics/values or trustworthiness. Every employee should have strong work ethics. It makes you do the right thing at the right place according to your moral code or professionalism even when no one is watching you. This enables others to judge how you will behave in a particular situation.

Leaders with strong *moral* principles help to foster high employee *morale*.

It is up to you to choose a set of moral rules and principles that will probably lead you to a happy and satisfying life. You have to check how you have lived your past life: have you adhered to these principles or have you lived without any moral guidance? You may have had failures, and others might have criticized you for the same. You are what you are today because of the way you lived your life. Own responsibility for what you are now. Make sure what is to be done to realign yourself to your moral principles.

There will be people who may try to advise you to give up your character or integrity, saying that nobody's perfect, and there is no meaning in being honest all the time. *But violating what you believe is right is the greatest attack on your character.*

Character formation and character building are to be focused if you want to develop integrity. Our schools earlier had a subject called moral science to inculcate moral principles in children; it has been removed later thinking that character building is primarily the duty of parents. Parents in turn are happy the way things are. They are after getting their wards admitted in prestigious institutions. Their only concern seems to be that children should get high degrees and become money spinners. Very few are concerned these days about good character formation. Without good examples from parents or teachers, students are left to themselves and they grow up impatient to grab anything and everything on their way without any regard for moralistic principles.

They are not given training to control emotions, to be agreeable, to be sociable and conscientious, to face difficult situations.
They do not know what is sacrifice, love, tolerance, trust-worthiness, help, respect, honesty. Each one is trying to surge ahead pushing others back without any consideration for others.

Many marriages fail and the society has lost its moral compass. Yes, the religious texts emphasize all these but the quest for the material has replaced such moral teachings.

All the scriptures mention that Pride, Greed, Lust Sloth, Envy, Anger ....are all cardinal sins. But who cares? We may be proud, angry, envious, greedy and slothful. Very little effort is expended to get rid of these that gnaw away at our otherwise good personality traits.

Pride

It makes one think of others as less worthy individuals and hence he/she is not enthusiastic, polite, considerate or willing to give compliments. A proud person is fully involved with himself that he soon falls flat on his face. Life will pass without him and he will be a loner fending for himself. A humble person, on the other hand, will go with the world and he will have plenty of friends.

Generally world does not think pride as a problem. How do we overcome something so sly?

Proud people treat others unfairly and they don't accept responsibility for wrong doing. They often speak more and listen less. They are concerned with themselves all the time.

Proud people may not really know all that they think they do. Let those who are proud think 'what is there to be proud about after all?' The greatest men and women have been humble. If they are not proud, why should ordinary guys like you and me be proud? Even if you have something more than the commoners, you should be thankful to the universal forces and feel more humble.

We are like bubbles just formed and will burst out in less than a second in the cosmic time scale. If you have real merit others will recognize it and give you due credit. Even then you have nothing to be proud of. Your inheritance, environment and your parenting bequeathed it upon you. Have a thankful heart and feel all the more humble.

Greed

Greed is nothing but the endless desire to get more and more things in life. Greedy people become blind and are ready to do anything to get the things they want. It can even lead them to become destructive. If you don't become aware of it and try to control it, your greed will only increase with each passing day.

Envious guys keep on craving for new things and they are generally never contended. Their craving will remain until their death and they will go from this world with unfulfilled desires and totally unhappy.

It's simply impossible to fulfil every person's wish on this planet. So we have to become contended with what we have. Greed can be controlled. You can control your desires, and yet live a happy, peaceful and satisfied life. *It can be experimentally proven that your mind tricks you to desire the objects you crave but you don't need all of them. May be all that you have now is quite sufficient and you may not want anything more.* Understand that your greedy mind is driving you to be crazy for more.

When you are greedy you only think about yourself and want more and more. Become kind to the people around you –those who are deprived of everything— and you will realize your folly and you will probably put a stop to your greedy attitude.

Even if you get everything you crave, your greed doesn't stop. Craving for more has simply become your nature. You cannot take anything when you go from here. Your happiness has nothing to do with how much you possess but how contended you are with what you have. *Becoming happy with what you have is an essential feature of a good personality.*

Lust

There are two forms of lust: lust for power and lust for carnal pleasures.

The sons of many rulers killed their own fathers to ascend the throne and grab power. There are so many high level executives who go out of their way to get promoted to a higher position.

Man would do anything to have sex with a chosen female. You need to control your lust; otherwise the unfulfilled desires will drive you crazy and will bring you problems one after another. Lust is like any other bad habit; it can be overcome with decision and persistence.

Learn to respect yourself and others. Avoiding drugs and alcohol seems to help in controlling lust.

Sexual feelings are very natural but it does not mean one can stoop to the level of animals to satiate the same.

- Acknowledge that you have issues with lust and then prepare yourself when you will be going anywhere with temptations.
- You can distract yourself by bringing the picture of a baby, moving with friends you love or getting engaged in something that will totally absorb your mind.
- If your lust is uncontrollable you get help immediately.

Sloth or laziness

Controlling one's energy level is not all within one's power. There is a lot of genetic propensity and hereditary determinants. This does not mean that one can be slothful so as not to develop his talents or find his rightful place. Each one should try to give his best in whatever profession he finds himself, develop whatever talent he has, become physically and mentally fit and be on the path of self-development.

If you are slothful in anything, ask yourself

- Am I tired?
- Am I overwhelmed?
- Am I afraid?
- Am I uninspired?
- Does grief or sadness affect you?
- Are you disorganized?
- Do you say often or at least at times 'I am lazy'; 'I am worthless'?
- Do you worry about all that stuff of tomorrow?

The difficult work is often smaller than what you imagine; you can get past it more easily than you think. Each one of the tough tasks has to be attacked on their own. There is no use in postponing things; the best time to do them is now. Otherwise you may not do it ever.

Envy

Being jealous of another who is better off than you will have a disastrous effect on your character and personality. Envious guys never see things in themselves; they go for comparisons. You will always find someone who is higher than you in what your mind is focused at the moment. It can spiral out of control into destructive jealousy or even depression.

Think how it harms you. You may not call a friend anymore as you think he has left you behind. You wish if you had his artistic ability, looks or smartness........It takes up your time thinking about him/her and where they have reached.

- Envy ruins your relationships;
- It creates so much negativity.

How do we overcome this nagging problem?

- Stop judging yourself so harshly. Your friend's career may have taken to new heights and yours has not. Be patient, your time will come. Further, you cannot be like him. You are two distinct individuals with their own personalities.
- Stop comparing. There is no meaning in comparisons 'that is better than this'-may not be always true. Stop lamenting on what you don't have. Focus on what you already have.
- Live by your own definitions of success. There is no point in comparing another with you. You are two distinct individuals who are unique. You cannot have what he has and he cannot have what you have.
- Just because you don't have ditto of what he has doesn't mean you are inferior or he is superior. Ultimately what matters is whether you are happy. He may not be happy with what he has. You can be happy with yours if you want to.
- Instead of being envious, start taking steps to get a better car/house/position/friend than your competitor.
- He may not be all that happy or great as you imagine. Maybe he isn't better off than what you really are.
- Stop comparing; focus on your talents and assets.
- Focusing on those who make your life full is a positive way to cancel out your feelings of envy.

The best way to deal with envy is to try to change whatever you can and pray to give you the courage to accept whatever you cannot.

Cultivate a grateful heart for what you have and spend more time with friends who have a similar attitude. Make a list of at least 25 things you can be grateful for.

- Stop complaining about the absence of anything for at least one day, then another and another...
- Start complimenting more people on their small or big achievements. It will help your mind stay positive.

- Why don't you try to help the deprived, those below poverty line or the physically handicapped ones?
- Accept you have envy and know the person you are envious of has flaws of his own too.

Anger— We have already discussed this in chapter 35.

Honesty is the best policy

Being honest is a great thing. Truth is very powerful. Telling lies is in no way going to help us overcome our problems. They will become harder with our lies.

Be honest with yourself before you try to be honest with the world. If you have done a mistake have the courage to accept it and own it. If you have failed you can always blame someone else and try to escape. But every successful person owns their failures and mistakes.

Honesty also implies that you do your duty well. Doing the bare minimum just to keep the job going is not an honest way. Give your best, and become truly honest to your job.

When someone at the counter gives you more cash than he should, give it back and help him. Through such simple acts you prove to be honest to yourself and your self-esteem simply doubles up.

If you have to speak a lie to help someone it may be better than the truth which will hurt him. This is perhaps the only occasion where you may opt to lie to help someone. Having the guts to say the truth will help you in the long run. There will be many opportunities that tempt you to be dishonest— refuse them with fortitude. It is good if you put in place a system by which you reward yourself when you are truthful so that it motivates you to do likewise again. A simple self-congratulation with 'well-done, keep it up' to yourself.

Chapter-39

Manage your time

"The bad news is time flies. The good news is you're the pilot."

—Michael Altshuler

Time Management is the art of doing more in a given period of time. It is a technique to save time and improve your productivity and life efficiency. It is an essential part of your character formation. You have 24 hours each day like the great people and you can use it to the maximum benefit or waste it.

Time management is essential to manage life in a creative and successful way. We all have a lot of things to be done; we do not get enough time to do all of them and we feel we are losing control in our lives. Many of the things we do have nothing to do with our goals or what is truly important in our lives. Still we all feel that we have no time. We sometimes feel we are going through life without really experiencing it. We all think life will slow down at some point and we will be able to manage time better. But it won't happen by accident. If we want the situation to change, we need to consciously implement time management principles listed below.

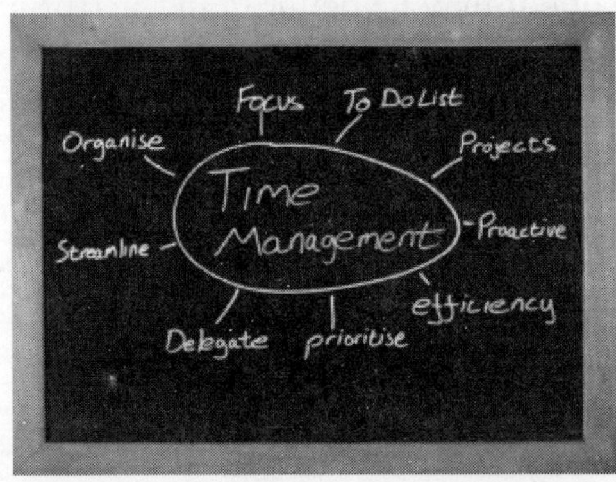

- Before we can make more time for things that really matter in our lives, we first need to identify what those things are. Set **clearly defined and specific goals**. You must examine your present situation and assess what goals are important and what action you need to take to achieve them. Break your goals down into discreet steps. Review your progress towards your goals. Cross the things off the list that are completed. And focus on those yet to be done.
- **Prioritize—** Focus on the urgent and important works now rather than on those that *are easy to do or unimportant.* Start with the most

important task first. Make a daily list of all the tasks to be done, say in a week. Prioritize items on the list as important/not important, urgent/non-urgent. Urgent and important tasks can be highlighted.

- **Become effective—** You can be efficient if you work hard and spend all your time on important tasks but you will not be effective. Also remember an urgent task may not be important at all.
- **Rewrite and prioritize your list on a regular basis**.
- **Keep a 'to-do list'—** Write it down every day— you should have a reminder system to tell you when you need to do what. Use your diary to write down the things you need to do, including appointments and deadlines.
- **Note down questions to ask** before meetings, or interviews. This helps you focus on important objectives. No one can hold everything in their heads.
- **Avoid distractions and interruptions** to your work. Keep your desk tidy, check emails at set points in the day and do not waste your time in social networks.
- **Organize your work**. Make a list to remind you of what you need to do and when, so as to meet deadlines.
- **Identify areas in your life when you will be wasting time**.
- **Develop a regular work routine** starting with the time you wake up and finishing it when you go to sleep.
- **Apply the Pareto principle of time management (80/20 rule).** In general, 20% of our effort produces about 80% of our results. This means that if we have a list of 10 things to do, two of those are likely to produce greater results than the other 8 put together. Try to identify which tasks really move you towards your goals and give those the priority they deserve. You will probably find that some of the lesser tasks no longer need to be done at all.
- **Know Tim Ferre theory of 4-hour work a week**. He wants us to strike out the non-essential aspects in our work schedule and focus only on items that have the highest value.
- **Haste makes waste.** Trying to do too many things in little time will boomerang. Give yourself sufficient time to do a job.
- **Avoid procrastination**. The best time to do something is usually now. Do the most unpleasant tasks as soon as possible. Rather than postponing things you don't really want to do, get them out of the way as soon as you can.
- **Persevere when things do not go right.** Things will not move smoothly as you progress. We need to become positive when there are failures and setbacks. Develop strategies (such as taking regular exercise, meditation and the like) to deal with pressure.

- **Focus on your most productive time of the day**. Some people work better in the mornings, and some are more focused in the evenings. Understand your best time and make use of it.
- **Take breaks to clear your mind and refresh yourself to refocus**. Allow time for fun and relaxation to refresh your mind and body. Have some time for yourself. After 45 minutes of focused effort, spend 10-15 minutes on something else which will relax your mind. This seems to be a good rule. After 45 minutes our ability to focus begins to taper off and we no longer perform optimally.
- **Delegate tasks**. You cannot do everything by yourself. Or, you cannot undertake to do more than you can. If you do, it may often result in stress and tension. Learn the art of delegating work to your subordinates as per their skills and abilities.
- **Avoid multi-tasking**. Most of us feel that multi-tasking is an efficient way of getting things done but the truth is that we do better when we focus and concentrate on one thing. Multi-tasking hampers productivity and should be avoided to improve time management skills.
- **Do not try to be a perfectionist**. There is no point in spending 90% of your time trying to make a less than 5% improvement. It's important we know when it is time to move on to the next activity. Perfection is not needed nor is expected.
- **Expect the unexpected**. Many things happen in your life and work which are not fully expected by you; be prepared for them and allow some time for the unexpected.
- **Start early**. Most of the successful men and women start their day early as it gives them time to sit, think, and plan their day. When you get up early, you are more calm, creative, and clear-headed.
- **Learn to say no**. If you say yes to all the request of your friends and colleagues you may not have time for essentials. Also refuse politely to accept additional tasks if you think you're already overloaded with work. Take a look at your 'To-Do' list before agreeing to take on extra work.
- **Give quality time to your family**. One who has a happy family life is at peace with himself and with the world. Hence include some quality time— one or two hours in the evenings – to spend with your spouse and children. Manage your job and family with equal importance.

- **Be flexible**. These are rules made for you and you need not be a slave to them. You are the best judge of your life and use your time as you feel best suited. But the above guidelines will help you in a positive way.

Parkinson's law states that work expands to fill time available for its completion. It implies if there is more time you will continue doing it, obviously at a lesser efficiency than when the time is less, until you complete the same. Implication: You will do the same job at a much less time if you are asked to. We all tend to go on doing less work and waste our precious time.

When our time is effectively utilized to harmonize with our goals, our work and family life becomes more fruitful, efficient and happy. We all waste a lot of our time and this hampers our success. There is a saying 'those who utilize their free time effectively will not remain at the bottom for long.' Keep track of how you spend your time and try to make use of all your wasted time. With effective time management skills you will feel you have enough time for everything in your life. **Remember what Ashley Ormon said: "You can't make up for lost time. You can only do better in the future."**

The most valuable component of our life is time. You may have heard that time is money. The truth is: time is life itself and the more time you have, more your life. If we learn to have a balanced view of how we use our time, life can be both enjoyable and productive. If by applying some of these time management tips you gain some time in your life—that is great; you become capable of creating more time.

You cannot be like a log of wood carried by the current and being taken here and there; you have to plan how you utilize your time and control it. You need to have life-goals and short-term goals to manage your time effectively. Have you written down your long-term and short-term goals? If not do it within a few days. Your short-term goals will dictate how you will spend your time on a daily basis. Identify the number of hours you waste each day. These hours should be fruitfully used to advance faster in your life, to make investments and improve your market value. Have realistic deadlines and make sure your deadlines are always met.

"Time is the most valuable coin in your life. You and you alone will determine how that coin will be spent. Be careful that you do not let other people spend it for you."

—Carl Sandburg

Chapter-40

Ten personality traits

1. Learn to say 'I am sorry'

Think: An apology is a way to take responsibility for one's past actions. It is common practice to seek apologies from the wrong-doers or to apologize when you wronged others. Apologies have a power to heal emotional wounds if they are properly done. An unhealthy or improper apology won't heal but may harm. The wrong-doer should apologize to make amends, usually by saying "I'm sorry"? Do not apologize simply because someone else expects it from you. You should feel the mistake and want to make amends. An apology is not merely to ask forgiveness. You are expressing your feelings that can contribute to the growth of the relationship and enhance the understanding of one another.

Reflect: Why do we not practise the two very powerful and irresistible words: "I'm sorry."

It takes nothing away from us to say these two words, yet they convey a lot. You might have heard: love is never having to say we are sorry, but sincere love is going to a person and telling him or her that we are sorry for what has happened, even if we are the one wronged. Justice may be our due when someone has wronged us but it is a sign of great virtue to say "I am sorry."

Decision: Learn to say "I am sorry" and make it a practice to see the difference it brings in your and others' lives.

2. Start with one step

Fact: A journey of a thousand miles begins with a single step but without making that first step, nothing will be accomplished. Once the first step is taken, the next one and the next and all the others may simply fall in line. You already have enough to begin with that first step. If you are looking for alibis or 'if onlys' you will never really start anything or reach anywhere. If you keep on thinking about the problems ahead, you may tend to postpone things. Prolonged delay paralyses your initiative. There is no auspicious day, there is no special circumstance; every day is right and every moment is auspicious. All the conditions will not be just right and perfect conditions will never arrive. What you can do now in the present set-up is all that really matters. The distant and the vague appeals to the human mind as no specific action need to be taken. It is difficult to take the first step but remember, you unleash a lot of power in doing so.

Reflect: From what I know of the lives of the great, I can tell you that everything great they achieved had begun with something very insignificant. And many people have not achieved anything simply because they failed to take that first step. The impossible is many a time the untried. If you are in grave doubt or worry about when or how to start the journey, just take the first step and get past the starting point. Subsequent steps would follow and you may reach a point of no return. You already have enough to take the first step and then the next.

Decision: If you have decided to do something, do not worry what will happen tomorrow. Take the first step and then the next and the next and go on.

3. Do it now

Fact: One of the most important qualities of anyone, who wants to succeed is 'do it now'. Time is a precious gift and the awareness of how you are using time to do, what you are supposed to do now is crucial. Do not postpone. Maybe the task is tough, complicated or unpleasant. Maybe you do not know how to do it or you feel you are hard pressed for time. But if you have the will to do, you will easily manage it: you can seek professional help, your decision will make it pleasant or you can break it into manageable tasks. If you have more to do time expands and it comes to your help.

Think: If there is something you need to do now, do it, because tomorrow you will have plenty of other things to do. The day after will bring more jobs. If you postpone things to be done now, they all will get piled up and you will be sorry. Regular postponing will erode your confidence levels too.

Action: Do what you are supposed to do today, toady itself. Before going to bed ask, "Have I completed all the tasks meant for today?" If not, decide to complete the list from tomorrow. Let, the unfinished ones of today be the number one priority of the next day.

4. Become grateful

Fact: We got life down here at these advanced levels of civilization. We have to thank nature but these are times when no one is content. The more one gets, the more one craves for. There is an insatiable demand for more wealth and material goods and naturally people are unhappy. Let us be content with whatever we have, let us be content with our circumstances. There are those who will be content if they have food, clothing and a roof to sleep. Insatiability will rob you of inner peace and the joy of living. You can be happy and content and then accept whatever life is gracious to give you. It is far better to be content with what we have than be disappointed at what we do not have.

Think: Shouldn't we cultivate an attitude of gratitude towards the universal forces that have decided to give us this life to our own parents, who gave physical expression to that decision and who loved and took care of us throughout our infancy and childhood, to all those good souls (relatives, neighbours, *et al.*) who loved us and to our teachers who enlightened our minds, and to all our friends and acquaintances and to every co-traveller in this great journey.

Reflect: Having a thankful mind and a grateful attitude is the springboard to mental happiness and personal success. Love is perhaps the greatest force that can attract anything to your life. Love can easily emanate from a grateful mind and without love one cannot succeed.

Decision: Become grateful to the Universe, family, teachers, neighbours, friends, acquaintances and all the co-travellers.

5. The universe wants us to succeed

Fact: It has given us enough to do so. We have the freedom to pass here unnoticed, unsung or even as a total failure. We have also the freedom to leave our mark, by succeeding in life.

Think: Benjamin Disraeli said, "Remember to nurture your mind with great thoughts for you will never go any higher than you think." It is also good to keep in mind what Jonathan Kozol has said, "Pick battles big enough to matter and small enough to win." Here is a big quote of Theodore Roosevelt which we shall remember every day of this year, "Far better it is to dare mighty things, to win glorious triumphs, even though checkered by failure… rather than to rank with those souls who neither enjoy very much nor suffer much because they live in a gray twilight that knows not victory nor defeat."

Reflect: Stephen Hawking was fully paralyzed. But his brain was intact and with this faculty he has become a top scientist in the world. He occupied Newton's Chair in Oxford University. We all have a working brain. We may not have the IQ of Hawking. But one of the nine intelligences (each one of us has them) will be good in us. It is up to us to soar up tapping this springboard.

Decision: Find out my innate aptitude and end up in a job or profession in harmony with it. If I do not enjoy my present work, I will say goodbye to it and search for something I will enjoy doing.

6. Leave your footprint

Fact: Ninety-nine per cent of all of us go from here leaving nothing for the posterity to remember us. No wonder they all forget we have ever lived down here. The bubble busted just like it formed, unknown, unheard, unsung.

Reflect: We can pass this life unnoticed but that is not what we have been brought down here for. There is an inner potency in each one of us to climb higher. The details of the climb are immaterial; let us decide now and here to make the climb. The mountain and the modus operandi and netiquettes of journey can be decided later but the decision to go up is very important.

Decision: Let us make up our minds to leave our footprints on the sands of time. Let us take a solemn oath that we will not let ourselves go from here without having achieved something, without becoming successful, without having helped a number of our fellow travellers. It may not be to the tune of those like Abraham Lincoln, Mother Teresa, Mohandas Karamchand Gandhi, Albert Einstein or Nelson Mandela. Our output may not be comparable to Shakespeare, Leonardo Da Vinci, Michel Angelo, Raphael, Picasso or Beethoven. Nevertheless we shall leave our imprint; we shall live a life of self-worth and happiness leaving something good which the posterity will remember us for.

7. Your appearance speaks

Fact: The external world responds to you the way you feel about yourself inside. The more confidence you feel about yourself, the better will be the treatment you get from others. The well-dressed person commands more respect and gets more positive responses. The shabbily dressed person is taken generally as careless, inefficient and is treated relatively badly too. Your appearance speaks.

Think: Everyone knows the value of dressing well for an interview and candidates generally take care. Those with the habit of dressing well would definitely appear better as they take extra care on the day. Many of us now understand that one's appearance and the ensuing "I am good" feeling helps one to perform better in any examination or interview or job.

Action Plan: Wear fresh clothes and shoes (at least use washed and pressed/ polished ones); comb your hair in the most pleasing way and apply perfume (if you like) after shaving, trimming your mustache (if you have one), removing unnecessary hair from face, pruning the nails of toes and fingers and taking time to shower and make your body immaculately clean. This is not only applicable on a special day; let it become a habit whether you are at home or outside.

8. Show empathy

Fact: Showing empathy genuinely is one of the most important interpersonal skills that anyone must really master. And what is empathy? Empathy is the capability to appreciate, understand, and accept another person's emotions. If someone tells you "I lost my job." Respond with empathy, and you will greatly improve your relationship with that person, but if you don't care, you would certainly ruin the relationship.

Reflect: If you are willing to make sacrifices for others as you move forward, you can be sure that those whom you help will reciprocate and the universe will return your services hundredfold. Share others' joys, triumphs, successes and sorrows. You can share with the others your successes and failures too. Through empathy you establish strong relationships which are essential for any success.

Decision: I am not living in an island. Without building strong relationships far and wide I cannot make the climb, and I will cultivate empathy with all I come across.

9. Simplicity

Reflect: Most people would like their lives to be simpler but they seldom move beyond this simple notion. Simplicity does not imply one has to be poor or lead a back-to-the-land lifestyle. Even complex lives can be made simple through creativity. There can be simplicity on the other side of complexity. Simplicity and success should go hand in hand. We long for a simple life when our life becomes more complex than we can handle. Through a step by step path we can achieve our goals or lead a simple life.

Action Plan: Concentrate as to how to achieve things in a simple way. Understand what is essential in any given situation and get the thing done without pomp and show. You can thus, conserve your energies and avoid unnecessary exertion and expenses. Lead a humble life reducing your expenses, loving your family and all you come across. Focus all your energies on your chosen line with a broader and comprehensive view of life and the whole universe. Rise above sectarian, parochial and religious sentiments. See the good in all and love each one. Live with lesser rules, with simple eating and exercise habits without a lot of paraphernalia. Live in a house of your liking, kept it clean and organized.

10. Cultivate positive thoughts

Fact: The person you are on the outside, is fully controlled by the one inside. Whereas the inside person is controlled fully by your thoughts, beliefs and attitudes. Choose the right knowledge and control your future and your destiny by controlling them. As Napoleon Hill states, your mind becomes magnetized with the dominating thoughts you hold. Choose your thoughts and attitudes that will propel you to success. Failure or success is a product of your mind and its dominant and sustained thoughts.

Decision: Read books of great people who have risen up from lowly positions fighting back all possible adversities. Mingle with positive-minded, ambitious, honest and hardworking people. Do not get into the trap of negative people who are fatalistic or who advocate that the society or government has to uplift you.